The Complete Guide to
Silk Ribbon Embroidery

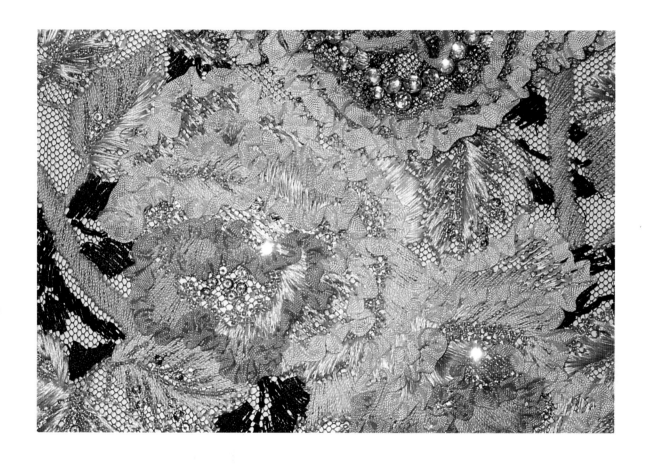

WATSON-GUPTILL ❧ CRAFTS

The Complete Guide to Silk Ribbon Embroidery

BASIC STEP-BY-STEP TECHNIQUES FOR MAKING BEAUTIFUL DESIGNS FOR WEARABLES, ACCESSORIES, AND HOME DECOR

Victoria Adams Brown

WATSON-GUPTILL PUBLICATIONS/NEW YORK

TO ALL WOMEN AND THE MAGIC IN THEIR FINGERS

If you'd like to contact Vickie Brown,
please write to her at the following address:
Shrieking Tree Farm
P. O. Box 416
Fountainville, Pennsylvania 18923

On page 1: This sumptuous blend of rococo ribbon, silk thread, and
various embellishments over black tulle netting is stitched on a silk
taffeta ballgown attributed to the Spanish couturier Balenciaga, circa
1950s. Courtesy of Maison Lesage. Photograph by Vickie Brown.
On pages 2–3: Using the work on page 1 as her inspiration, the author
stitched an elegant composition of pink, white, and black on a pink ground.

Senior Editor: Candace Raney
Edited by Joy Aquilino
Designed by Areta Buk
Graphic production by Hector Campbell

First published in 1996 by Watson-Guptill Publications,
a division of BPI Communications, Inc.,
1515 Broadway, New York, N.Y. 10036

Library of Congress Cataloging-in-Publication Data
Brown, Victoria Adams.
    The complete guide to silk ribbon embroidery: basic step-by-step
techniques for making beautiful designs for wearables, accessories,
and home decor/Victoria Adams Brown.
        p.   cm.
    Includes index.
    ISBN 0-8230-0795-2 (pbk.)
    1. Silk ribbon embroidery.   I. Title.
TT778.S64B76   1996
746.44—dc20   96-10205
                                            CIP

Manufactured in Singapore

First printing, 1996

1 2 3 4 5 6 7 8 9 / 04 03 02 01 00 99 98 97 96

ACKNOWLEDGMENTS

The following individuals deserve more than words from me. I only hope that time allows me to return their favors.

My sincere thanks to Candace Raney, senior editor at Watson-Guptill Publications, for offering me such a wonderful opportunity, as well as the opportunity to work with the best. As developmental editor, Joy Aquilino was a tremendous aid to me while assembling the manuscript, and skillfully arranged my stitch designs and words into thoughtful, easy-to-understand progressions. Designer Areta Buk's magic touch resulted in a visually beautiful book that entices the beginner and entrances the intermediate stitcher.

A special thanks to Monsieur François Lesage and Madame Francoise Tellier for their hospitality while I attended Ecole de Broderie d'Art Lesage in Paris. Monsieur Lesage was exceedingly gracious in the time he spent with me, in allowing me to tour his *atelier* and to photograph the beautiful samples in his archives and for recounting stories that mesmerized this author. I would also like to extend my gratitude to Kaethe Kliot of Lacis in Berkeley, California; Veronica Patersen of *Piecework* magazine; Wilanna Bristow of San Antonio, Texas; and Liz Dircksen of Angelsea in Stockton, California, for sharing information with me.

The beautiful photographs and projects that enhance the historical section of this book were made possible through the kindness of Heather Joynes, one of Australia's finest ribbon embroidery teachers and authors; Myra Walker at the University of North Texas in Denton, Texas; and Susan Schlack at the Moravian Museum of Bethlehem in Bethlehem, Pennsylvania.

My appreciation to the following manufacturers, which contributed their products for use in this book: Bucilla, WFR Ribbon, Wright's Ribbons, and Novtex, for ribbons, braids, and trims; DMC, Coats and Clark, and Kreinik, for floss and specialty threads; Zweigart, for damask fabrics; Adhesive Technologies, for glue guns; Samara Bros., Inc., JanLynn Corporation, and Wimpole Street Creations, for clothing blanks; and Pres-On Products, for adhesive-backed cardboard shapes.

I am fortunate to have had the opportunity to work with the following women, who added beautiful touches to my designs. Rebecca Bennion produces exquisite hand-dyed variegated ribbons that enhance any project with the good fortune to be stitched with her silk. My good friend Barbara Quast designed and produced the wonderful polymer clay vase featured in the framed Dresden vase project (page 98). Her ability to translate my crude sketches and telephone instructions far exceeded my expectations.

The following women aided me in carrying out my day-to-day affairs and the nuts and bolts of completing the book, and I am eternally grateful for their help. Sue Keiffer makes it possible for me to maintain my work and travel schedules by kindly loving and taking care of the farm and all the animals. Cynthia Greb gives me healing space among my 16-hour days. Maureen Cox, an exceptional seamstress, can read my mind and stitch my models with a minimum of guidance. Susan Alderfer and all the technicians at the Pro-Slide Shop in Lansdale, Pennsylvania, capably guided me during my photography sessions at their facility.

I would like to express my appreciation for the continued support of all the students I have had the pleasure to teach. Among them, I am the student; every class teaches me new lessons and gives me energy and inspiration.

I thank my friends Patsy Moreland, Judy Kipke, and Jacqueline Till for their wisdom, insight, listening abilities, and all their years of support.

Living with a creative person on a good day is a challenge at best. Far too often my deadlines impact my partner's life, and to him I extend my utmost appreciation and indebtedness for his patience and support. Thank you, Michael.

Contents

Introduction

While on a trip to London several years ago, I spent a delightful evening with a new acquaintance from Sydney, Australia. For years I had owned a children's apparel manufacturing company, and my customers appreciated all the one-of-a-kind hand-dyed, handpainted, and embellished clothing my staff and I created. I told my companion that although I wanted to investigate a new creative undertaking—silk ribbon embroidery—I couldn't find a source for supplies. She then showed me photographs of her daughter's wedding gown, which was heavily embellished with silk ribbon flowers. The combination of traditional embroidery techniques with the luster and opulence of the ribbon evoked a timeless elegance. I knew immediately that I had to try my hand at this craft.

Silk clothing is desirable for its softness, sheen, and the luxury of wearing beautifully cut and draped fabric; the same holds true for silk ribbon. Its luster, delicacy, and dimension give traditional embroidery stitches—which are usually worked in thread or yarn—a completely different look. Although the intricate appearance of the stitches can at first be intimidating, I soon discovered that silk ribbon embroidery is easy to master. Since it employs traditional stitches, ribbon embroidery quickly becomes second nature to anyone who has ever stitched, even if she hasn't picked up a needle in decades. The simplicity of the stitches and the relatively short time required to complete projects also put silk ribbon embroidery well within the reach of the beginning stitcher. Compared to thread and yarn, silk ribbon's width covers an area of fabric more quickly and effectively, requiring just a fraction of the time to complete an embroidery design. Because it is so smooth, silk ribbon flows easily through a wide variety of fabrics.

Silk ribbon embroidery creates a classic, nostalgic style that is becoming increasingly popular as we embark on the 21st century, in which we must strive to balance the ever-increasing momentum of the future with the creative achievements of the past.

HOW TO USE THIS BOOK

The Complete Guide to Silk Ribbon Embroidery demonstrates for the beginning or intermediate stitcher how to create elegant projects with silk ribbon by using a combination of twenty embroidery stitches. The book begins with a detailed survey of the elements of the craft, from ribbons, flosses, and embellishments to stitching and pattern transfer tools. To ensure your stitching success, the first chapter also includes indispensable advice on organizing materials, preparing ribbons and fabrics for stitching, and laundering, ironing, and storing projects. Central to the book is the stitch guide, which reviews silk ribbon's handling requirements and demonstrates the stitches with detailed instructions and step-by-step photographs.

The remaining chapters present twenty-five projects arranged in four categories: accessories, wearables, home decor, and special occasions. The projects were designed to offer stitchers an opportunity to create beautiful objects while meeting the demands of a busy lifestyle. Accompanying the step-by-step instructions for each project are its three requirements: level of stitching skill (either beginner or intermediate), amount of time needed to complete it, and stitching supplies, including ribbon yardage. With these helpful features, you can make informed decisions about how to budget your time and money, and plan to embroider a blouse for an upcoming social function or stitch a beautiful heirloom for a special shower or wedding.

Although the list of supplies for each project reflects the item that is shown in the photographs that also accompany the instructions, you can adapt the palette of ribbon to fit your personal preference. For example, if a design is stitched with several shades of peach but you prefer mauve, simply work with light, medium, and dark shades of mauve, then choose complementary shades of blue, yellow, and green as accent colors.

DEVELOPING YOUR STITCHING SKILLS

As you continue to develop your ribbon embroidery skills, I recommend that you purchase books and videotapes and attend classes and workshops. Books illustrate new stitching styles and unusual combinations of color and form. Classes provide students with knowledge and energy. Every opportunity will reveal new possibilities.

Be selective when choosing a teacher. Remember that she is a student with a few more classes under her belt who is still learning and perfecting her craft. Without your presence, interest, and enthusiasm, she wouldn't be teaching a class in the first place. The students I am fortunate to work with always end up teaching me and renewing my energy. Inevitably, the prevailing theme of a beginning ribbon embroidery class is the students' lack of self-confidence. By the end of the class, however, they are immersed in learning a new craft and enjoying the creative possibilities ribbon embroidery has to offer. So as you read through this book, realize that you are not alone in beginning a new endeavor, and that your efforts will eventually yield generous dividends.

Silk ribbon embroidery is truly "goof-proof." Stitching is much like handwriting in that every individual stitches distinctly. Your project won't look exactly like the one in the photograph because yours is imprinted with your special energy. The satisfaction experienced while stitching and the sense of accomplishment derived from completing a project are the two most important "techniques" this book has to offer. For you to enjoy stitching—being lost in the moment, creating and taking pleasure in the creation—is what this book is all about. And each piece you stitch will increase your skill and self-confidence, until you are ready to add your own special touches to your projects.

And once you've completed a project, sign and date it, noting why or for whom you stitched it. (If you're stitching a garment, stitch a small tag with this information to an inside seam.) While conducting research for this book, I frequently examined embroidery by unknown stitchers who couldn't imagine that their work would survive to be appreciated in a future century. So as a gift to posterity, document your projects as you stitch.

A BRIEF HISTORY OF SILK RIBBON EMBROIDERY

Embroiderers today can find boundless inspiration in the rich and varied history of decorative stitching. It is most likely that the development of this art form paralleled that of weaving and garment-making. As human culture evolved, embroidered clothing helped to express economic, social, and religious status, and was used over the centuries to identify rank and authority in all walks of life. Nevertheless, power and wealth were not the only messages that embroidery could convey.

Women often lived severely restricted lives, and their needlework became personal diaries of their unfulfilled longings. An intensely personal craft, embroidery continues to hold the same emotions and aspirations shared by stitchers over the centuries.

Silk's arrival in the West is shrouded in myth. It is believed that the Chinese began cultivating silk nearly 1,500 years before the birth of Christ. Legend has it that in the mid-6th century A.D., two Nestorian monks smuggled silkworm eggs and white mulberry seeds out of China to Constantinople by hiding them in hollow bamboo canes. These eggs, which were successfully hatched under artificial conditions, enabled Justinian I (483–565) to establish a thriving sericulture (silk cultivation) throughout Europe. Until the mid-1700s, all European silkworms were descended from those legendary eggs.

The story of silk ribbon embroidery is woven from four threads of development that reflect its most important spheres of influence: France, England, Australia, and the United States.

FRANCE

Silk was first used to produce ribbon in the late 15th century, in Bologna, Italy. In 1517, ribbon production shifted to Saint-Etienne, southwest of Lyon, France, where it eventually reached its height in the late 19th and early 20th centuries.

France became a dominant force in women's fashion in the 17th century, when Louis XIV (1638–1715) patronized and promoted the art of embroidery. In the

An example of silk and silk ribbon embroidery stitched by Michonet in the late 19th century. Courtesy of Maison Lesage. Photograph by Vickie Brown.

Detail of an ivory and black satin ballgown by Pierre Balmain (French, 1904–82) featuring ribbon embroidery, circa 1950. Courtesy of the Texas Fashion Collection at the University of North Texas, Denton, Texas.

Monsieur François Lesage displays his interpretation of Van Gogh's Sunflowers *for the 1988–89 Yves Saint Laurent Collection. Courtesy of Maison Lesage. Photograph by Vickie Brown.*

early part of the century, narrow, shaded silk ribbons were applied to the bottoms of skirts to mimic swags of flowers, a technique known as *broderie de faveur.* By the mid-18th century, exquisite stitching, frills, and trimmings embellished the gowns of aristocratic and wealthy women, echoing the lavish interior decoration of the French Rococo. For nearly a century after the French Revolution, embroidery was generally restricted to military uniforms and adorned women's clothing only on ceremonial occasions, as it was associated with the frivolous excess of the royal court.

The 19th century heralded the dawn of the Industrial Revolution and the rise of the bourgeoisie. Although this era spawned technological advances in the garment industry, including the development of embroidery, cutting, and fitting machines, the nouveau riche spurned cheaply made, mass-produced goods, demanding sumptuous attire that was beyond the reach of the local dressmaker and the patterns she adapted from the fashion gazettes. Enter Charles Frederick Worth, an Englishman who emigrated to France in 1845 and became the first *couturier,* or fashion designer, in 1858. Realizing that decorative embroidery would satisfy his customers' hunger for extravagance, Worth and his young embroiderer, Michonet, started an avalanche of hand-embellished fashion that lasted from 1860 to 1914. Worth's house flourished and his popularity soared, especially after he created gowns for Empress Eugénie, wife of Napoleon III. The lavishness of Michonet's embroidery was matched only by the extravagance of the lives of Worth's clients. Typically, these women changed gowns four to five times a day, and embroidery was always an essential ingredient of their attire.

Michonet produced *rococo* (rosette-embroidered) ribbons finished with seeded fringing, a great accomplishment at the time. A gown could require 300 hours of embroidery, with a single button taking up to 10 hours. Designs incorporating ribbon embroidery were invariably floral and stitched with China ribbons (a term commonly used to describe 1/8-inch ribbons shaded from one edge to the other, regardless of where they had been woven). Designs consisted of roses, daisies, and forget-me-nots executed in tiny straight stitches and ribbons *ruched,* or gathered, to form circular flowers.

In 1924, Albert Lesage (1878–1949) purchased the House of Worth and renamed it Maison Lesage. Lesage and his wife worked with some of the greatest fashion designers of the 20th century, including Balenciaga, Balmain, Schiaparelli, and Vionnet. In 1949, their son François became director of the company, and over the years he collaborated with Chanel, Dior, Givenchy, Lacroix, Saint Laurent, and Valentino to create sparkling, heavily embroidered, wearable jewels. Today, Maison Lesage also houses the impressive archives of Lesage et Cie, which document over 125 years of French haute couture with 60,000 samples of embroidery. The photographs on the opposite page and on page 1 illustrate the romantic florals of the 19th century, and the soft, feminine treatments of the 1950s that best represent the silk ribbon embroidery of that era.

ENGLAND

Silk ribbon embroidery made its first appearance in England in the early 17th century, when London dressmakers began copying the French technique of *broderie de faveur.* Following the restoration of Charles II in 1660, the art of decorative embellishment ran rampant. Gowns were regularly festooned with ribbons in bows, rosettes, bunches, and loops. In the 18th century, ribbon embroidery adorned waistcoats, lingerie bags, decorative aprons, and most notably large workbags that were carried by all fashionable Englishwomen. The style of China ribbonwork that was popular in France at that time was also stitched in England. Rococo floral bouquets arranged in baskets and cornucopias tied with flourishing bows were fashionable motifs. Aerophane, a stiffish silk gauze, was folded, tucked, and stitched down to create large flowers, while chenille, silk, and metallic threads were used to stitch stems and tendrils.

In the early 19th century, ribbon colors became brighter, and the backgrounds darker and richer. Ribbon embroidery was worked on dresses, men's waistcoats, and purses, as well as on table runners and mats, portable screens, and mirrored frames. In 1880, the rococo technique was revived following the invention of the "Pompadour," which was similar to China ribbon but dyed in a wider range of colors. By the 1890s, backgrounds were lighter and more luxurious—silk, satin, chiffon, and lace—and two new large-scale ribbons were introduced: the ½-inch crinkled "giant crepe," and the picotee, a ⅝-inch ribbon available in plain and shaded versions with a deep ruby serrated edge, which was used to make carnations.

In the early 1900s, tastes in flowers, backgrounds and colors shifted once more. Designs featured tiger lilies, dahlias, and other multipetaled flowers; linen, felt, bengaline silk, moiré, and velour were popular backgrounds; and color combinations were dazzling; for example, orange poppies on a green velour ground, or royal blue cornflowers on chrome silk. By 1930, ribbonwork was applied primarily to girls' party dresses, kimonos, cushions, table runners, tea cozies, and screens. Although ribbonwork has never been at the forefront of English embroidery, in that tradition it continues to be associated with fashion, frivolity, and femininity.

This elaborate basket of flowers, which was fashioned from French ombré lettuce-edge ribbon, adorns a gold silk chiffon dress with layered ruffles and three rows of matching gold lace inserts, circa 1925. Collection of Vickie Brown.

"Basket of Flowers," stitched by Australian needleartist and author Heather Joynes for the 1994 Embroiderer's Guild National Seminar. Courtesy of Heather Joynes.

AUSTRALIA

In Australia, ribbonwork has been in fashion at various times over the past 250 years. In the early years of Australia's settlement, needlework was a necessary, time-consuming chore as well as a constant companion to women isolated from social interaction. In the early 19th century, the invention of the sewing machine and the growth of leisure time among the burgeoning middle class increased the popularity of women's genteel handicrafts or "fancywork." Fancywork items were often sold at fashionable bazaars to support charitable causes, but never as a business venture.

Art de Brodeur, published in France in 1770 by Charles Germain de Saint Aubin, was consulted by many Australians who wanted to keep abreast of current fashion. This book shows many items that were heavily embroidered with ribbon. At the end of the 18th century, small ribbon-embroidered bags known as "indispensables" or "reticules" were designed to hold the "necessities" that the slender fashions of the day couldn't accommodate. A costly wardrobe accessory, pins were used frequently in the 18th and 19th centuries, making embellished pin cushions useful gifts.

The China ribbons that were fashionable in England and France in the 18th century reached the height of their popularity in Australia in the early to mid-19th century. Giant crepe, picotee, and pompadour ribbons arrived later, and were used through 1910 on such items as tea cozies, pillow shams, cushions, and handbags. In the 1920s and 1930s, ribbon embroidery patterns appeared in instructional booklets and magazines featuring designs for children's wear, lingerie, and evening bags.

Because the supply of silk ribbon to Australia ceased during World War II, ribbon embroidery techniques languished until the 1980s. Today, ribbonwork is extremely popular in Australia, and accomplished Australian stitchers such as Jenny Bradford and Heather Joynes have been instrumental in reviving the craft in the United States, inspiring thousands of American women with their beautiful, traditional techniques and practical instruction.

THE UNITED STATES

Starting in the colonial era—as early as the mid-17th century in Virginia—several attempts were made to establish a sericulture in America, all of which failed. In the late 18th century, Ben Franklin tried unsuccessfully to raise funds to establish a silk-producing venture in Pennsylvania. In 1826, the introduction of a superior species of mulberry tree revived an interest in sericulture in Philadelphia. Unfortunately, this "silk craze" was short-lived, as the trees could not withstand Pennsylvania's harsh winters.

In spite of these early failures, there were several successful American silk enterprises throughout the 19th century. Beginning in 1827, the Harmonists of Economy, Pennsylvania, a celibate religious community, developed methods to maximize the amount of silk fiber that could be reeled from a cocoon and produced silks that rivaled those from England and France. By the early 1850s, the combined effects of the technological advances of the Industrial Revolution, strong competition from foreign textile manufacturers, and the Harmonist's aging population brought their venture to an end.

In 1855, Brigham Young, governor of Utah Territory, initiated a sericulture by ordering a supply of mulberry seeds from France. With a labor force consisting of mainly of women, children, and the elderly, the Mormon pioneers built a cottage silk industry that flourished from 1860 to 1900. As the prices of textiles manufactured outside of Utah fell, so did the price of silk, leading to the eventual collapse of Utah's silk trade.

Throughout the tumultuous years that Americans labored to develop a silk industry, American silk ribbon embroidery—always considered to be among the most elegant of that needleart—made occasional yet significant appearances. In 1741, Moravians migrated to the colonies from present-day Bosnia-Herzegovina and established a community in Bethlehem, Pennsylvania. In 1750, a Moravian women's organization known as the Sisters of Bethlehem founded the Seminary for Female Education, which is still in operation today. Contrary to the prevailing notion that a pursuit of the ornamental arts would help attract potential suitors, the Moravians believed that instruction in the needlearts was part of a well-rounded education, and that silk ribbon embroidery should be stitched to thank God for the skills He gave to create beauty. The students' fine needlework was acclaimed throughout America, helping to establish the seminary's reputation as a center for culture and education. Between 1785 and 1840, the seminary's enrollment exceeded 2,000, and its students, who ranged in age from 15 to 20, hailed from 24 states and 6 countries. These young women stitched silk and satin dresser scarves, purses, and trinket boxes with silk thread and silk chenille ribbon and embellished them with gold seed beads.

The Sisters of Bethlehem contributed significantly to the history and aesthetic development of silk ribbon embroidery, and today Moravian-style needlework can be found in museums, private collections, and antique shops. The seminary's most celebrated piece, which was presented to First Lady Mrs. John Quincy Adams in 1826 and is now in the collection of the Adams National Historic Site in Quincy,

Detail of a silk sash embroidered with cocoon silk, circa 1860. Collection of Vickie Brown.

Massachusetts, is a large floral wreath of crepe, silk ribbon, silk floss, and chenille stitched on a black silk ground. The photograph below shows a similar composition stitched by a seminary student.

After a brief lapse, silk ribbon embroidery re-emerged in the late 19th century. Articles heralding its durability and resistance to fading were published in needlework, home decor, and fashion magazines. As they are now, consistent dye lots and colorfastness were important concerns. At that time, silk ribbon embroidery was used to embellish quilts, dresses, and a variety of personal accessories.

In the early 20th century, original design motifs and inventive stitch combinations became the hallmarks of American silk ribbon embroidery, though the tried-and-true background fabrics of silk and satin remained unchanged. During this period, the most popular silk ribbon colors were deep shades of mauve, claret wines, and deep blue-greens. Silk ribbon embroidery was used to commemorate epic airplane flights in 1926 and 1927. In 1937, Mrs. Theodore Roosevelt, Jr., brought silk ribbon embroidery national attention when she stitched designs on a trifold table screen with a background of blue silk.

World War II and the subsequent development of synthetic fibers created a long hiatus for American silk ribbon embroidery. Although American dollmakers had been knitting and crocheting with several widths of Japanese silk ribbon since the early 1980s, silk ribbon embroidery was revived only after the "Australian invasion" in 1990. The variety of styles and techniques of today's American needleartist illustrate the vast creative potential of this elegant craft.

Framed silk ribbon embroidery on black silk, circa 1800, stitched by seminary student Anna Salome Heckewelder Rice (1784–1857). The German inscription reads: "Der Herr segne und behute dich" (The Lord bless and keep you). Courtesy Moravian Museum of Bethlehem, Bethlehem, Pennsylvania. Photograph by Michael Brown.

Getting Ready to Stitch

The material requirements for a silk-embroidered project are fairly simple: ribbon, thread or floss, a few embellishments, needles, fabric, hoop, and scissors. Before you begin your silk ribbon odyssey, however, you should understand the elements of the craft and be familiar with all the creative and practical options that are available to you. Most of the items discussed in this chapter can be purchased at fabric, craft, and hobby stores. If you can't find a local retail source for your supplies, or if you can't find something that's used in one of the projects in this book, consult the source directory (pages 142–143).

Silk Ribbon

Standard silk ribbon widths (from top): 2mm, 4mm, 7mm, and 13mm.

Lustrous, tough, and elastic, silk is a protein-based natural fiber that is spun by the silkworm to construct its cocoon. Not only is silk stronger than any other natural fiber (as well as most synthetic fibers, with the sole exception of nylon), but a length of silk thread is 1.4 times as strong as a steel filament of the same dimensions.

Silk is cultivated primarily in Japan, China, and other countries in the Far East where the mulberry tree, whose leaves are the exclusive diet of the silkworm, grows in abundance, and where the labor required to produce silk is relatively inexpensive. Although silk has been cultivated for over 3,500 years, most Westerners still find it mysterious. This is due in part to the fact that silk has been an imported commodity in much of the West since the mid-1920s. At the start of World War II, the silk supply to the United States evaporated virtually overnight, and silk's availability in the U.S. remained sparse through the late 1980s. The huge void caused by silk's absence in the intervening years prompted American manufacturers to develop synthetic fibers such as nylon, acrylic, and polyester for the commercial textile market.

As a result of an ever-increasing interest in natural fibers, stitchers have discovered silk ribbon's favorable working properties as a stitching medium. Because so little information about silk is available, many negative myths still persist. Novice silk ribbon stitchers inevitably express concern about silk's alleged fragility, troublesome laundering requirements (contrary to popular belief, all silk can be handwashed in lukewarm, soapy water), and scarcity.

To satisfy the demands of the ribbon embroidery renaissance, manufacturers and distributors such as Bucilla Corporation, Ribbon Connection, WFR Ribbon, Inc., and YLI Corporation have made silk ribbon both affordable and readily available, in a range of widths and colors and in reasonable yardage quantities. Silk ribbon is currently available in three forms: standard, variegated, and bias-cut. A variety of synthetic ribbons can also be used with silk ribbon embroidery techniques.

Both silk and synthetic ribbons can be obtained through a wide variety of retail sources. Silk and synthetic ribbons can usually be found at large craft, hobby, and fabric chain stores, while smaller needlecraft and quilt shops tend to carry only silk ribbon. For more information, refer to the source directory, pages 142–143.

STANDARD SILK RIBBON

The photograph above, left, illustrates the common widths in which silk ribbon is produced. The 2mm width is excellent for small-scale projects such as jewelry, and perfect for stitching small flowers and buds. In part because it is the easiest to work with, the 4mm width is currently the most widely used and is available in the broadest range of colors. The 7mm width is suitable for larger and more dramatic stitches, though its handling (and that of wider ribbons) differs slightly from that of 4mm silk ribbon. (The 4mm and 7mm widths are used in all the projects in this book. See "Working with Silk Ribbon," pages 32–33.) The most expensive and hardest to find, the 13mm width can cover large areas extremely quickly and makes lavish, beautiful flowers. Regardless of its width or color, silk ribbon is light and radiant, with a luxurious *hand,* or feel.

After stitching a project or two, you'll want to investigate other types of silk ribbon. Note that while only standard silk ribbon and a few synthetic ribbons are used in this book, it's important to be familiar with all the creative options that are available for stitching.

VARIEGATED SILK RIBBON

Used by stitchers since the early 19th century, variegated silk ribbons are hand-dyed with two or more colors. (Another kind of variegated ribbon, *ombré ribbon*, is dyed with several shades of a single color.) When you stitch with variegated silk ribbon, your flower's petals will change colors or shades dramatically without having to re-thread the needle. Variegated synthetic ribbons, which are just as beautiful as silk, have recently entered the marketplace.

BIAS-CUT SILK RIBBON

Bias-cut ribbon is made by cutting a length of white silk at a 45-degree angle to its edge, then dyeing it in a variety of color combinations. This cutting method creates an unsealed edge that drapes less delicately than standard silk ribbon and is resistant to crushing and folding. Available in an assortment of widths and weights, bias-cut silk ribbon is heavier than standard silk ribbon, and therefore more suitable for stitching large, striking flowers.

The open-cut edge on a bias-cut ribbon won't unravel but will fray slightly, creating a "vintage" look that is highly desirable among crocheters and knitters. To encourage bias-cut ribbon to fray, simply prick the edge of the ribbon with the needle before stitching. This technique is often used to stitch irises, in which the feathered edge of the ribbon creates the bearding that is characteristic of those flowers.

SYNTHETIC RIBBON

While nylon, polyester, and acrylic are all used to produce synthetic ribbons, the brand of synthetic ribbon that is most similar to silk ribbon is Heirloom Sylk, which is manufactured by Mokuba, a Japanese company, and distributed in the U.S. by WFR Ribbon, Inc. Made of Azlon, a microfiber derived from a milk by-product, Heirloom Sylk has a slightly wiry texture that is common to all synthetic ribbon, resulting in sharp, spiky angles instead of soft curves. However, from a distance, and to an untrained eye, this product closely resembles silk ribbon. Mokuba also manufactures a beautiful array of specialty synthetic ribbons and tapes—organdies, metallics, and variegateds—that add texture and sparkle to designs worked in silk.

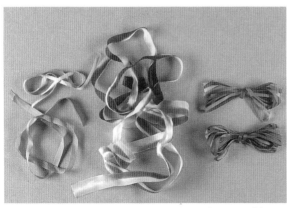

(Left to right) Standard silk ribbon in 4mm and 7mm widths, bias-cut silk ribbon, and variegated silk ribbon.

A selection of 7mm synthetic ribbons (left to right): cross-dyed luminous, organdy with gold metallic edging, organdy, and variegated synthetic ribbon.

Threads and Flosses

Silk ribbon stitches can benefit immeasurably from the visual contrast provided by threads and flosses. Delicate stems, vines, and leaves stitched in thread or floss lend subtlety and softness to silk ribbon flowers and can help support an overall design, which might otherwise seem to float on the surface of the fabric.

In contrast to thread, which is usually sold on spools and worked in single strands, floss is sold in four- and six-strand skeins and worked in multiple strands. (In this book, flosses are worked in two, three, or six strands.) The variety of threads and flosses currently on the market offers stitchers endless creative possibilities. Each of the products described below is available in a myriad of colors.

- *Embroidery Floss.* Typically produced in 50-yard skeins, this matte-finish floss is made of 100 percent cotton. Embroidery floss can be substituted for any of the flosses and threads listed below. Both Coats & Clark and DMC manufacture high-quality brands of embroidery floss.
- *Marlitt.* This rayon floss has a very high sheen. Available in four-strand skeins, marlitt is usually worked in two, three, or four strands. Distributed by Coats & Clark, Anchor is a premium brand of marlitt.
- *Metallic.* Metallic thread has a distinctive sparkle rather than a glossy sheen. It is available in spools, in light, medium, and heavy weights, as well as in a broad "braid" width. Kreinik, Sulky (pronounced SUE-kee), and Madeira all produce good-quality metallic threads.
- *Perle Cotton.* Made of 100 percent cotton, perle cotton is a low-sheen twined thread available in four widths, from 12 (the thinnest) to 3 (the widest). Size 3 is used, for example, when stitching a large stem for a 13mm silk ribbon flower. Size 8 is similar in width and character to silk buttonhole twist (see below), and if necessary can serve as a satisfactory substitute. DMC and Coats & Clark are both reliable manufacturers of this product.
- *Rayon.* This type of floss, which is similar to marlitt but not as shiny, is unusual in that it is typically worked with one strand. It can usually be found in specialty sewing and quilting stores. Divine Threads is a notable brand of rayon floss.
- *Silk Buttonhole Twist.* The beauty and high luster of this 100-inch filament silk thread add elegance to any project. Silk buttonhole twist can be difficult to find and is expensive, but the effect it produces is well worth the investment. Kanagawa (pronounced kah-nah-GAH-wah) and Tire are the primary sources for this product in the United States.

(Left to right) A skein of six-strand embroidery floss, two skeins of marlitt, a card of silk buttonhole twist, and two sizes of perle cotton thread: a skein of size 3 and a ball of size 12.

Embellishments

Finishing touches such as buttons, beads, charms, and other embellishments serve several important functions in silk ribbon embroidery. In addition to highlighting a design's principal elements and enhancing its textural interest, these objects have highly reflective surfaces that produce depth and radiance within a design.

If you're an avowed collector, becoming a silk ribbon stitcher will give you ample opportunity to satisfy your collecting impulse, since you'll always be on the alert for embellishments. You can find buttons, beads, and charms at sewing and crafts stores, where you can buy individual embellishments as well as large plastic buckets and bags of assorted buttons. There are also many mail order companies that specialize in sewing embellishments. But the best and most interesting places to look for these items are antique stores, where vintage treasures can be unearthed, sometimes for relatively low cost. Regardless of where you look, you'll find a variety of shapes, sizes, materials, colors, and finishes.

For instance, charms, which are often made of or finished with a metallic material, are available in a wide range of shapes and can have either a polished or matte (sometimes referred to as "antique") finish. Available in iridescent, "pearlized," and frosted finishes, glass beads and faux pearls are generally sold according to size, either small, medium, and large, or by metric units (4mm, 8mm, 12mm, and so on). The term *seed* is used to describe the tiniest beads and pearls.

With such abundant variety, it's easy to let your enthusiasm for these delightful adornments run away with you. When making your selections, however, you should let the scale of the stitch design be your guide, rather than your general preferences for color and size. As with the stitches themselves, you should also consider the application; for instance, large beads may not be appropriate for a garment you plan to wear (and thus launder) often.

Most embellishments require only a beading needle and a single strand of floss to be incorporated into stitching. Beading needles come in a range of lengths, all of which feature a tiny eye (a needle threader is recommended). Sizes #7 and #10 are used with most of the projects in this book (see page 23).

A card of antique cobalt blue oval glass buttons, buttons in imitation mother-of-pearl, jade, ivory, and coral, and several brass charms.

An assortment of beads in a variety of shapes, colors, and finishes.

Stitching Tools

Part of silk ribbon embroidery's appeal is that it requires relatively few tools. A selection of needles, a pair of scissors, and a hoop are usually all that a beginner needs to stitch her first project.

NEEDLES

The needles used to stitch a ribbon embroidery project are chosen on the basis of three criteria: the width of the ribbon, the nature of the fabric, and the way that the stitches are being worked. There are several categories of needles, each of which includes a range of lengths and eye sizes. Within each category, a needle's size is indicated with a number: the higher the number, the smaller the needle.

The needle's eye must accommodate the ribbon's width and make an opening in the fabric large enough to pull the ribbon through. There are no hard-and-fast rules as to which kind of point a stitcher should use. In general, sharp-pointed needles are used with heavyweight or tightly woven fabrics, or when a stitch requires that the fabric be pierced repeatedly. Designed to prevent snagging, blunt-pointed needles are recommended for use with loosely woven fabrics.

- *Chenille needles,* which have sharp points and large, oval eyes, are essential for silk ribbon work. It's a good idea to have an assortment of sizes on hand, from #18 to #26. A #26 is suitable for 2mm and 4mm ribbons, a #24 for 7mm ribbon, and a #18 for 7mm, 9mm, and 13mm ribbons. The largest sizes—#13, #14, and #16—are used with organdies, synthetic ribbons and tapes, and the exceptionally wide 32mm ribbons, although they are sometimes difficult to find in sewing and notions stores. These sizes of chenille needle also make excellent laying tools, to eliminate twists and curls in the ribbon so that stitches are uniform and attractive. (See "Working with Silk Ribbon," pages 32–33.) Tightly woven fabrics like denim, twill, fleece, taffeta, moiré, and velvet should all be worked with chenille needles.
- *Tapestry needles,* which aren't as heavy as chenille needles, have large eyes and blunt points.. Traditionally used for needlepoint and cross-stitch, tapestry needles are also used as laying tools. A range of tapestry needles in sizes #22 through #26 is recommended. Use #24 and #26 for heavier fabrics and #22 for more delicate fabric work.
- *Embroidery needles* are used with thread and floss. Select an assortment of sharps from #3 to #9.

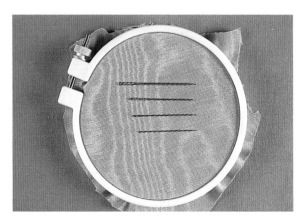

Standard ribbon embroidery needles (from top to bottom): a #18 chenille needle, a #24 tapestry needle, a #7 embroidery needle, and a #10 beading needle.

- *Beading needles,* which have tiny eyes, are used to stitch beads, pearls, and charms to fabrics. Depending on the bead size, use a sharps #10 or a #7, which is a shorter needle that can also be used for embroidery.

In contrast to other types of embroidery, a thimble is not recommended for use with silk ribbon, as it would very likely impede your handling of the ribbon.

SCISSORS

A pair of small embroidery scissors with sharp blades is an indispensable stitching tool. I keep several sharp pair of scissors in my studio, two pair in my traveling bag, and one small Swiss Army knife with scissors in my purse. Because ribbon embroidery is so portable, I attach tassels to the handles of my scissors to prevent them from slipping under the cushions of couches, airplanes, and car seats. To avoid stressing or fraying the ends of your ribbons with anything less than clean, sharply made cuts, buy the most expensive scissors your budget will allow, and use them *only* to cut ribbon or fabric. Maintain the blades' sharpness by honing them on a sharpening stone or by having them professionally sharpened.

EMBROIDERY HOOPS

Whenever possible, you should mount your project on an embroidery hoop. A hoop holds fabric taut and flat so that your fingers are free to manipulate the ribbon, and keeps the rest of the fabric from interfering with your stitching.

I prefer to use good-quality wooden German hoops that are specifically designed for machine embroidery. These hoops will last a lifetime, and their hardwood frames will never form rough edges that can snag ribbon or fabric. Because they are thinner than regular hoops, they make it easier for the stitcher to reach the center of the stitching surface. A 3- to 5-inch circumference is recommended, with a 4-inch circumference allowing for the most efficient manipulation of the ribbon. The tension in a wooden hoop is adjusted by turning the screws on the upper stave. Wooden hoops can be purchased at most craft and fabric stores.

Designed to prevent the wrinkling that often occurs with a wooden hoop, a Q-Snap consists of a rectangular plastic frame that supports the fabric from below, and four plastic sleeves that clip onto the frame over the fabric to keep it in place. The tension is adjusted by shifting the sleeves with a flick of the wrist. The entire assembly quickly snaps apart for easy transport. Available in a variety of sizes, a

(Top) Gingher's 5-inch Tailor's Points/Craft scissors, the finest knife-edge, chrome-plated shears on the market, make sharp, clean cuts and come with their own sharpening stone. (Bottom) Mundial ornamental 4-inch lightweight embroidery scissors.

large Q-Snap is particularly useful for stitching large-scale projects, as it provides a generous view of the stitching surface. Q-Snaps are generally found in smaller sewing and quilting shops.

Of course, there are some projects and surfaces for which a hoop is not appropriate, such as hats, small areas of garments like lapels and collars, and delicate, lightweight silks, which could become stretched or misshapen. As a result, these projects take longer to stitch. If you must work lightweight silk on a hoop, wrap the staves with yarn or surgical tape. To avoid snagging delicate fabrics on rough fingers, wrap the tops of your thumbs and index fingers with surgical tape.

PATTERN TRANSFER TOOLS

When transferring a pattern to fabric, always try to make as few marks as possible, rendering any marks you do make with a light touch. For simple designs, a series of dots lightly marked with a water-soluble marking pen should be adequate. The following pattern transfer tools are available in most sewing shops.

- *Fade-Away Pens.* These pens are best suited to simple projects that can be completed in one sitting. Depending on the fabric, a design can last up to several hours before the purple ink fades away. (Note that fade-away pens are generally not suitable for use with damasks, as the ink tends to vanish within minutes.) Any marks that remain after stitching can be removed with a damp cloth or cotton swab.
- *Water-Soluble Marking Pens.* These blue pens work well for marking simple designs on light- and medium-colored fabrics. When touched with a cloth or cotton swab dampened with cold water, the marks should dissipate. If the marks reappear (as they sometimes do), simply retouch them with a second application of cold water. Washing a garment in cold water after stitching ensures that the marks will disappear completely. Never machine-dry or iron a project that has visible trace marks, as some markers are set by heat into fabric.
- *White, Yellow, and Silver Fabric Pencils.* These pencils are designed specifically for marking dark fabrics. Keep points sharp and sketch very lightly. Use a fabric eraser to remove any marks left exposed by ribbon or floss.
- *Tulle Netting.* This method, which is often used to transfer entire designs, has never left a mark on any of the various fabrics I've worked with. Trace the pattern on a sheet of tracing paper with a permanent black fineline marker. Lay a piece of tulle netting over the traced pattern, then trace it on the netting with the

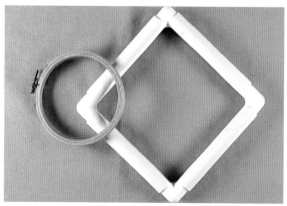

A 4-inch wooden embroidery hoop (left) and an 8-inch Q-Snap plastic stitching frame (right).

A fabric eraser, a double-ended fabric marking pen (one nib dispenses water-soluble ink, the other fade-away ink), and yellow and silver fabric marking pencils.

black marker. Pin the netting to the fabric, then use water-soluble marking pen to outline the pattern. Remove the netting and begin stitching. When stitching is complete, remove any visible marks with a damp cloth or cotton swab.

- *Iron-On Transfer Pens and Pencils.* These are especially useful for transferring a single design to several surfaces. Use an iron-on transfer pen or pencil to trace a pattern on a sheet of tracing paper, lay the traced pattern face down on the fabric, then iron according to the manufacturer's instructions. (Note that this method reverses patterns.) Each tracing yields up to twelve impressions. To continue using the pattern, simply retrace it with the transfer pen or pencil. Although the marks made by some iron-on transfer pens and pencils are semi-permanent and can usually be removed with cold water and a mild laundry detergent, it's safer to treat them all as if they were permanent.
- *Iron-On Transfers.* This type of transfer requires careful handling. (As with iron-on transfer pens and pencils, the design is always reversed.) Inks and instructions vary from manufacturer to manufacturer, but basically the pattern is permanently transferred to the fabric by means of a hot iron. You must have a steady hand, and work quickly and with a light touch. If the iron is held over the pattern too long the ink may dissipate, and the fabric can scorch if the iron's setting is too high. If you lift the edge of the pattern, you might accidentally reposition it and leave a double impression. If any of the pattern is left exposed after you're done stitching, you can cover it by embellishing the design with additional stitches, or you can try to remove it with cold water and a mild laundry detergent.
- *Dressmaker's Carbon.* This tracing method is very convenient, but it isn't recommended for use on delicate or vintage fabrics. Place a sheet of dressmaker's carbon ink side down on the fabric, lay the pattern over the carbon, then firmly trace its outline with a pencil. After stitching, remove marks either with water or a fabric eraser following the manufacturer's directions. It should be noted that these marks are sometimes difficult to remove completely.

MISCELLANEOUS SUPPLIES

As you leaf through this book looking for projects that appeal to you, you'll notice that some materials lists call for items that aren't used exclusively for stitching.

- *Batting,* which consists of multiple layers of cotton, polyester, or wool, is customarily used to line quilts.
- *Beading wire* is an extremely lightweight wire that can be easily cut with scissors. Available in 50- to 100-yard lengths, this all-purpose craft and hobby item can usually be found in the floral supplies sections of crafts or fabric stores.
- *E6000* is an industrial-strength permanent glue and sealant that provides superior adhesion on wood, metal, ceramic, glass, and plastics. Although its adhesive bond sets within 10 minutes, it requires 24 hours to cure completely.
- *Fray Check* is a clear, quick-drying liquid seam sealant that is applied to ribbon ends and to the cut edges of fabrics that have a tendency to ravel. Machine-washable and dry-cleanable, Fray Check is recommended for finishing the ribbonwork on all wearables. Because the slippery texture of silk and synthetic ribbons can cause knots to untie, it's a good idea to apply a dot of Fray Check to the soft knot at the end of a threaded 4mm ribbon before you begin stitching.
- *Glue guns* are useful for adhering embellishments such as pearls, braided trims, tassels, and laces, and for assembling projects. Always use a low-temperature glue gun and low-temperature glue sticks, as their high-temperature counterparts can damage your materials. Note that the glue dries almost immediately, so you need to work relatively quickly.
- *Polyester fiberfill* is used to stuff pillows, dolls, and other home decor items.

In addition to practicing your stitching, there are several things that you can do to make your projects more successful and your experience stitching with silk ribbon more enjoyable.

ORGANIZING YOUR MATERIALS

It's no fun feeling overwhelmed by your supplies. Rather than proclaiming the existence of unfettered genius, disorganization can put an irritating crimp in your creativity. If you find that you're continually stopping your work to hunt for what you need, consider putting a temporary hold on your project and take the time to organize your materials.

When starting a project, thread all the colors of ribbon and floss on the needles you'll be working with and stick them in a pin cushion. This saves a considerable amount of ribbon and time. After a project is complete, clip ribbons that are 8 inches or longer out of the needles and organize them by color in resealable plastic bags. Punch a hole in the top right- or left-hand corner of each bag, then run a large binder ring through the holes to keep the bags organized. These odds and ends might be appropriate for small projects, or they can be shared with another beginner. Protect your ribbons, fabrics, and laces from the negative effects of dust and direct sunlight—a powerful enemy of all natural fibers—by storing them in large, stackable plastic boxes.

Twelve-drawer plastic chests on casters are ideal for storing stitching supplies. Wheel them right next to your drawing board or worktable, or store them behind your favorite stitching chair. The compartments within each generously sized drawer can be used to sort flosses, threads, and ribbons by type and color. Use the other drawers to hold beads, pearls, extra scissors, hoops, marking pens, and tracing paper. If your collection of embellishments is overrunning your current setup, purchase a unit with 20 or 30 smaller drawers at a hardware store. For just a modest investment, these chests make it easy to organize a variety of items and allow the continued and orderly growth of your ribbon embroidery inventory.

SAFE STITCHING

While many artists and crafters must concern themselves with the toxic ingredients or by-products of their media, such as gases, fumes, dust, or chemicals, stitchers are free from such anxieties about fabric, silk ribbon, and most of the other elements of needlecraft. Embroidery work, however, does have a few potential hazards, though they can usually be offset by taking some simple precautions.

Embroidery can place undue strain on hands and wrists, neck and shoulders, and eyes. By providing support for hands and wrists, craft gloves can be particularly effective in reducing hand stress common to needlework. Handeze, a therapeutic craft glove developed by a New England research group, provides relief from a variety of continuous-motion hand and wrist disorders, including fatigue, arthritis, tendonitis, and carpal tunnel syndrome. Available at most craft, hobby, and fabric stores, Handeze gloves can also be used while performing other repetitive manual tasks, such as working on a computer or gardening.

Sitting with your neck bent forward for long periods of time will virtually guarantee discomfort and fatigue in your neck and shoulders. Make it a habit to get up and move around frequently to stretch your neck and back. Raise your hoop and hands by supporting them with several pillows in your lap, or try working your project on an embroidery stand, either a tabletop version or a standing model where the hoop can be positioned over your lap while you're seated.

To reduce eyestrain, always work in a well-lighted area. Eliminate distracting shadows by illuminating your project directly, which will also allow you to easily distinguish similar colors and shades of ribbon.

TESTING RIBBONS FOR COLORFASTNESS

Though ribbon colors rarely bleed or run, it only takes one ribbon dyed with a fugitive color to ruin a project. To ensure against such a calamity you should test all your ribbons for colorfastness, but note that dark reds, burgundies, and deep greens are more apt to run than most other colors. After you've gained some experience, you'll quickly learn which colors are more likely to be fugitive.

To test a ribbon for colorfastness, dip a 6-inch piece into a cup of clear water, or dampen it with water and lay it on a paper towel. If traces of dye are visible in the water or on the paper towel, add 1 cup of white vinegar to 4 gallons of cold water, soak the whole length of ribbon for about an hour, then rinse until the water runs clear. (To save time, place the ribbon in an old sock and machine-wash it separately in cold water on the delicate cycle.) Put the ribbon into a lingerie bag and dry it in the dryer on the fluff setting for 10 or 15 minutes. Before using it, retest a small piece of the ribbon for colorfastness. If the color still runs, do *not* use the ribbon.

PREPARING FABRICS FOR STITCHING

Before you can begin stitching, you must prepare your fabrics and garments by preshrinking them and testing them for colorfastness. This prevents shrinking and bleeding and keeps ribbon embroidery from puckering or popping the first time you wash an item. This step also removes the sizing that is used to treat many fabrics, making them easier and more pleasant to work with.

If the fabric or garment is sturdy and machine-washable, wash and dry it first. If you're working with linen, moiré, or silk, handwash the fabric and let it air-dry. The damasks I used for the projects in this book are a blend of natural and synthetic fibers, so it wasn't necessary for me to preshrink them; however, I did wash them to remove the sizing.

LAUNDERING SILK-EMBROIDERED PROJECTS

One of the most persistent myths about silk is that it must be dry-cleaned.Due to the recent advancements in cleaning agents, silk ribbon embroidery can easily be machine-washed or handwashed as well as dry-cleaned.

The cleaning schedule for a silk-embroidered item can vary widely, depending on how the item is used. For small accessories and home decor items, an occasional spot-cleaning or seasonal cleaning is sufficient in most cases. For wearables, natural fibers such as cotton, wool, and silk should be laundered frequently to remove salts and acids from perspiration. For synthetic fabrics, it's best to spot-clean a garment if it's been worn on just a few special occasions for short periods of time.

Machine-Washing and -Drying. If its fabric is machine-washable, a silk-embroidered item can be washed separately in cold water on the gentle, delicate, or wool setting, all of which have short agitation cycles. To keep the item from being pulled out of shape, place it in a lingerie bag or pillowcase (fasten the open end of the pillowcase with safety pins). If the fabric can be machine-dried, leave the item in the lingerie bag or pillowcase and dry it for 20 minutes on the "air only" setting. (Note that overdrying can damage the silk fibers.) Machine-drying tends to fluff and soften fabrics, minimizing the need for ironing.

Handwashing and Air-Drying. Gently handwash delicate and vintage fabrics in lukewarm water with a mild soap such as Ivory Snow, Quilter's Soap, or Washing Paste. Gently agitate the item, but don't wring it. The item can be drip-dried or rolled in a towel to remove excess moisture, then air-dried by laying it flat on another towel or by placing it on a padded hanger.

Dry Cleaning. If the dry cleaner is given special instructions, silk-embroidered items can in some cases be commercially dry-cleaned with excellent results. Note, however, that heavily embellished and highly dimensional stitching can be crushed or distorted by dry-cleaning equipment.

IRONING

Carefully press your fabrics or garments before stitching to straighten the grain of the fabric, and after stitching to remove wrinkles and hoop marks. If possible, use a Velvaboard when ironing your finished projects. Made of heat-resistant bristled nylon pile, a Velvaboard is a 9- × 19-inch latex-coated folding mat with a Teflon backing that captures steam and reflects it back onto the fabric. Simply lay the project face down on the Velvaboard and hold the steam iron slightly above the fabric. The wrinkles will disappear, leaving the proportions and shapes of the stitches intact. If you don't have or can't find a Velvaboard, a fluffy towel makes a satisfactory substitute.

A doll-size ironing board is excellent for pressing small projects such as cushion covers, sachets, and purses. You can order a doll's ironing board from Mini Magic, which is listed in the source directory.

STORING YOUR PROJECTS

Acid is the enemy of all natural-fiber fabrics—silk, cotton, linen, and wool—causing them to discolor, decay, and eventually disintegrate. Many people believe that in spite of efforts made to preserve their original condition, textiles naturally turn brown over time. In fact, it is the acids absorbed by a fabric's fibers that cause browning and staining to develop. These acids are present in the air as well as in the fumes released by ordinary paper products and unpainted or unsealed wood and wood products.

As your stitching skills improve, you'll want to protect your work to ensure that it remains in good condition so that your family and friends can enjoy it for years to come. When storing special keepsakes and heirlooms, wrap them in acid-free tissue papers and store them in acid-free boxes. Unlike standard papers and cardboards, acid-free paper products don't emit acid fumes as they age, thus providing an excellent environment for both long- and short-term storage of all natural-fiber fabrics and safeguarding against "acid rot," the common cause of natural-fiber fabric decay. (*Never* store natural-fiber fabrics in plastic bags or dry cleaner bags, as these also emit harmful fumes as they deteriorate.) Acid-free boxes also offer safe storage for papers, photographs, quilts—virtually anything you hope to pass on to loved ones. Mini Magic, a mail-order source for acid-free paper products (see the source directory), offers a conservation kit that includes materials and instructions for using acid-free papers, boxes, and cleaning solutions. By storing them properly, you ensure a future for the heirlooms you create.

Wearables need special attention. Wedding dresses, costumes, and other special garments should be dry cleaned or carefully laundered to eliminate traces of perfume, perspiration, body oils, and to remove food and drink stains. If stains are not immediately removed they will become permanent and worsen with time. Christening gowns should be washed immediately to remove milk or formula, which can sometimes take several years to develop into visible stains. Sodium perborate, an all-fabric bleach, can sometimes remove or lighten these stains, especially on white cottons and linens. To help reduce creases and ease folds, lightly stuff garments with acid-free tissue paper before boxing them.

DESIGNING A RIBBON EMBROIDERY PROJECT

The most difficult ribbon embroidery skill to teach is design, simply because individuals see, experience, and express their responses to the world differently. I tell my students that the creativity and artistry they use to plant a flower garden, decorate a room, or even pull together an attractive ensemble for a special gathering are also used to combine and arrange stitches in a beautiful silk ribbon embroidery design. The elements of creativity are different, but the creative process is the same.

With time and experience, design becomes effortless, and the skills that you develop will be honed with every project. I always carry sketchbooks with me so I'll have an organized place to compose my thoughts. I designed the projects for this book either by sketching directly on fabric, or by simply starting to stitch and watching the design develop. For the wearables, I tried on each piece of clothing and sketched the design on the garment while standing in front of a mirror.

If you're a beginning silk ribbon stitcher, you should concentrate on how to manipulate the ribbon for your first few projects instead of struggling to design an "ideal" arrangement of silk ribbon stitches for an object or garment. In more than one sense, silk ribbon embroidery is a free-form needleart: Not only is it frequently used to create graceful asymmetrical designs, but it is also unconstrained by strict rules and conventions. It's important to note that because every stitcher works silk ribbon with a different degree of tension, there is no "standard" way to stitch. Once you've gained some experience, you'll feel confident enough to change designs to include a few more lazy daisies, or to supplement with some French knots. In addition, many of the designs consist of "fantasy flowers" that eliminate the pressure of having to portray actual flowers. As you develop your technique and continue to add stitches to your embroidery "bank," you'll automatically embellish a ribbon embroidery design to suit your own taste.

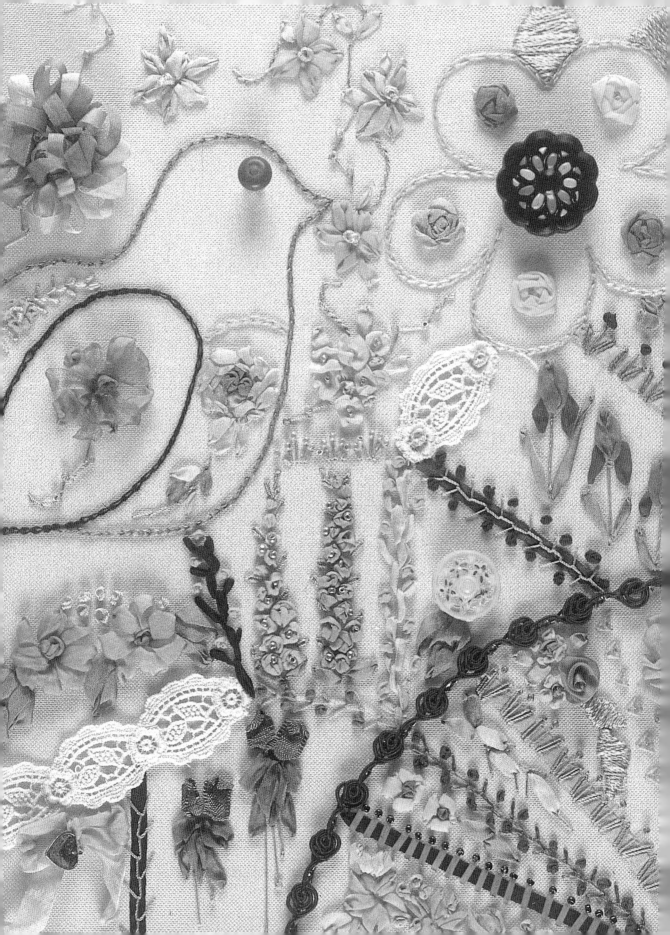

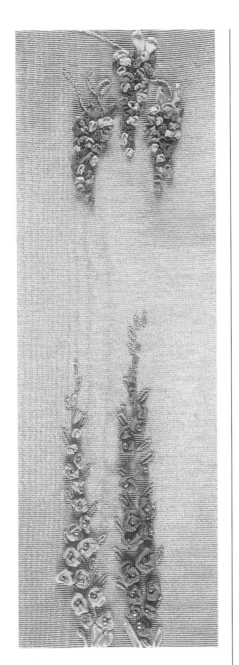

Silk Ribbon Stitch Guide

This chapter begins with a review of the basic handling requirements and working properties of silk ribbon, including the procedure used to thread a needle. In addition, this chapter demonstrates twenty simple stitches, many of which are basic embroidery stitches that have been used for hundreds of years. These are grouped into three categories—flat, knotted, and looped—and combined in a fourth category to create beautiful dimensional roses. Within each category, the stitches are arranged from easiest to most challenging, and relationships between stitches are noted in the accompanying text. The step-by-step photographs offer detailed progressions of each stitch, with the final photograph in each sequence showing the specific stitch in context with others. Wherever possible, examples are shown in both ribbon and floss.

Working with Silk Ribbon

The ribbon widths used in most of the projects in this book are 4mm and 7mm. Not only is the 4mm width easiest for beginning stitchers to work with, but it is also the most widely available.

To control silk ribbon's natural tendency to twist and curl, you should thread the needle with 12 to 14 inches of ribbon, a length that can be maneuvered with little difficulty. As you gain experience and skill, you can try working with 16 inches of ribbon, which will allow you to make several stitches before having to re-thread the needle. (Use shorter lengths when working with wider widths of ribbon.) The technique you use to thread the needle will depend on the width of the ribbon you're working with. See "Threading and Locking the Ribbon," page 34.

Occasionally, when a length of ribbon is too long, the weave of fabric too tight, or the fashioning of a stitch distorted, silk ribbon (and, less frequently, synthetic ribbon) can *fray*. This undesirable phenomenon is different from the feathered edges that can be produced on bias-cut silk ribbon (see page 19). On 4mm ribbon, fraying appears as small loops or picots along the edges; on 7mm and wider ribbons, the fibers separate, or *stripe,* creating an unsightly stress line down the middle. Both of these problems make stitchwork look worn and tired. If your ribbon begins to fray, remove the stitches and discard the frayed ribbon, then cut the ribbon out of the needle and re-thread it with a shorter length.

Other factors can increase a silk ribbon's potential to fray. Concentrated dyes used to make highly saturated or bright silk ribbon colors, low-quality silk fibers, and antiquated looms can all affect a ribbon's stitching performance. If one color of ribbon continues to fray despite the fact that you're using a shorter length, switch to another color.

MANIPULATING SILK RIBBON

Silk ribbon's need for dexterous handling is one of the primary differences between traditional embroidery worked with thread or yarn and silk ribbon embroidery. For many beginners, the impulse to dominate the slippery, twisting ribbon can be frustrating; however, it shouldn't be necessary to constantly adjust the ribbon to make it lay properly. While most of the stitches used in this book

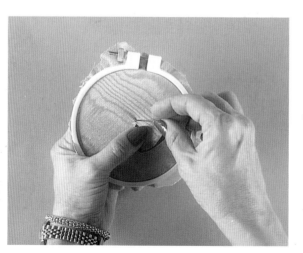

Reduce twists and curls by using the thumb of the hand in which you're holding the hoop to keep the ribbon flat against the fabric. As you pull the needle back through the fabric, guide the ribbon with your thumb.

require that the ribbon remain flat or untwisted, you'll probably only need to use your thumbs and index fingers to ensure that it remains straight as you work. By practicing your silk ribbon stitches, you will unconsciously learn to manipulate the ribbon.

Use the thumb of the hand in which you're grasping the hoop to hold the ribbon flat against the fabric. Then, as you pull the needle back through the fabric, tighten the ribbon over your thumb to ensure its smoothness. When the ribbon becomes twisted, use a *laying tool* to fix it. You can use practically anything as a laying tool—the eye end of a large, blunt needle, a toothpick, or even the needlework tool specifically manufactured for this purpose—as long as it accomplishes the objective: to eliminate the twists and curls on the front of the fabric so that subsequent stitches are uniform and attractive. Insert the laying tool into the loop of the ribbon and pull the ribbon up through the fabric several times. The twists in the ribbon will ease out as the ribbon slides over the tool. Once the twists have been removed, you can complete the stitch.

FINISHING YOUR STITCHES

Some experienced embroiderers assume that the messy appearance of the reverse sides of their silk ribbon projects means that they are stitching incorrectly. In fact, the criteria for "finishing" the back of a silk ribbon embroidery project are different from those for cross-stitch and other traditional embroidery techniques. There are very few hard-and-fast rules on this point. In general, silk ribbon shouldn't be dragged more than 1 inch when moving from one stitch to another. Excess ribbon, which may cause an unsightly bulge beneath the fabric, can also get in the way of making subsequent stitches and creates opportunities for the stitches to be pulled or caught, especially on wearables.

When stitching is complete, secure all the ribbon ends by tying them off with a soft knot, by weaving them under other stitches (this can be done while the needle is still threaded; just take care not to snag the previous stitches), or by tacking them down with two tiny straight stitches using embroidery floss in a matching color. Trim off any excess. Use Fray Check to finish the ribbon ends on all your wearables (see page 25).

As long as the stitches are secure and there's a minimum of "bulk" showing through the face of the fabric (left), it's permissible for the reverse of your silk ribbon embroidery project to look a little messy (right).

Threading and Locking the Ribbon

When threading a needle with 4mm silk ribbon, the ribbon is locked into the eye of the needle and a soft knot is formed in its tail. Locking this width of ribbon into the eye prevents it from slipping out of the needle, so that the ribbon has to be cut out of the eye when the stitches are completed. When the knot creates an unsightly bump beneath the surface of the fabric, leave a 1-inch tail at the end of the ribbon, then pierce it with a re-threaded needle to begin the next stitch.

In contrast, 7mm ribbon is simply inserted through the needle's eye and left unknotted, and a ¹/₂-inch "tail" is left on the back of the fabric with the first stitch, which is anchored in place with the next stitch. If 7mm ribbon were locked and knotted, the act of pulling it through the fabric would cause it to stripe.

Regardless of which width you use, always cut the ribbon at a 45-degree angle for easy insertion into the eye.

1. Pull approximately 3 inches of ribbon through the eye of the needle, then pierce it about ¹/₂ inch from the end.

2. Gently pull the long tail of the ribbon until the pierced piece locks over the eye of the needle.

3. Pierce the long end of the ribbon approximately ¹/₂ inch from its end.

4. Make a short running or basting stitch by gathering approximately 1¹/₄ inches of the ribbon onto the needle. The ribbon will appear to be draped in a circle. If the basting stitches are too short, the knot will pull through the fabric.

5. Slide the basting stitches over the needle and the eye to the bottom of the ribbon.

6. The soft knot that results will prevent the ribbon from falling out of the needle or pulling through the fabric. You are now ready to begin stitching.

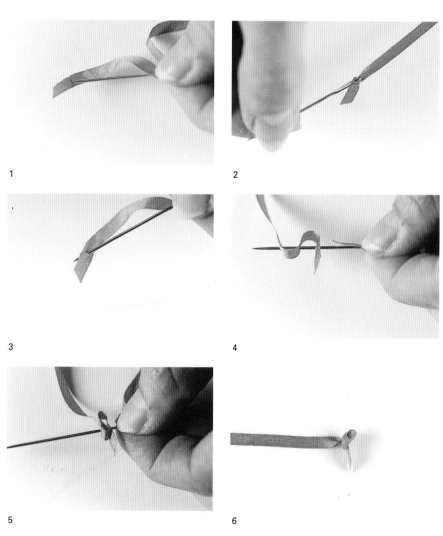

1

2

3

4

5

6

Flat Stitches

1. Come up at point A and go down at point B, making sure that the ribbon isn't twisted. The stitch should lie flat on the surface of the fabric when the ribbon is pulled through.
2. A completed straight stitch. The look of the stitch will vary according to the degree of tension used to pull the ribbon through the fabric. If a padded straight stitch is desired, proceed to step 3.
3. To make a padded straight stitch, come back up through the fabric a slight distance away from point C, then go back down the same distance away from point D.
4. A completed padded straight stitch.
5. A padded straight stitch tulip with twisted Japanese ribbon stitch stem and leaves.

The simplest of all embroidery stitches, flat stitches are produced by working the needle and ribbon in and out of the fabric. As their name implies, most of these stitches lie flat against the fabric when complete.

STRAIGHT STITCH AND PADDED STRAIGHT STITCH

The straight stitch is the most elementary of all flat stitches. It can be used singly to create a small bud, overlapped in a circle to make a rose (see page 48), or "padded"—layered with a second straight stitch—to make a full, evenly shaped petal.

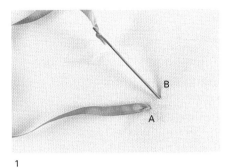

1

2

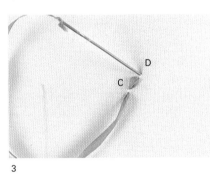

3

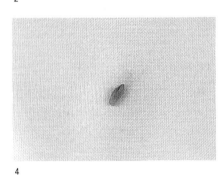

4

5

1. Come up through the fabric at point A. Untwist the ribbon so that it lies flat on the fabric. Insert the needle into the center of the ribbon approximately 1/4 inch away from point A.
2. To form the characteristic curl of the completed stitch, pull the needle through the ribbon slowly and gently.
3. Japanese ribbon stitch flower with French knot center and Japanese ribbon stitch leaves.

JAPANESE RIBBON STITCH

The Japanese ribbon stitch is extremely versatile. Not only is it possible to vary the lengths of the stitches and the degree of tension used, but stitches can also be layered using two widths of ribbon. Except for the straight stitch, the Japanese ribbon stitch is the easiest to execute and an enduring favorite among beginning students. Use single stitches for blades of grass or leaves, and layered stitches for flowers and buds.

1   2   3

TWISTED JAPANESE RIBBON STITCH

Frequently used to make dimensional petals and leaves, this stitch is similar to the Japanese ribbon stitch except that the ribbon is twisted before it is pierced with the needle.

1. Bring the needle and ribbon through the face of the fabric. Twist the ribbon loosely either once or several times, depending on the desired effect.
2. Pierce the ribbon with the needle, pulling it slowly through the fabric to create a curl at the end of the stitch.
3. A completed twisted Japanese ribbon stitch.
4. Blue columbines with twisted Japanese ribbon stitches in 4mm lavender silk ribbon.

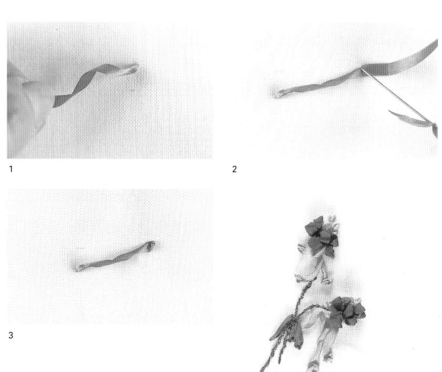

1   2

3

4

SATIN STITCH

Essentially a series of parallel, side-by-side straight stitches, the satin stitch was traditionally used with floss to create letters of the alphabet, names, or monograms. When stitched in silk ribbon, it can cover large areas quickly. Use it to fill in shapes, such as an animal's body, a landscape element like a path or a lake, or a large bow on a baby blanket.

1. To make a single satin stitch, simply come up at A and go down at B.
2. Repeat step 1 to lay a second satin stitch directly beside the first.
3. Continue adding stitches until the shape has been filled in.
4. Satin stitch leaves made with embroidery floss and 4mm and 7mm silk ribbon.

1

2

3

4

STEM STITCH

The stem stitch, which is usually used to outline rather than fill in a shape, consists of stitches that overlap at half-point intervals to make a continuous line. Both the length of the stitches in any given line and the side on which you work the stitches must be consistent. Always keep the ribbon or floss *beneath* the needle when making each stitch.

1. Come up at point A. Then, working in the opposite direction, go down at B and come up at C, keeping the ribbon or floss on one side of the outline.
2. Again changing direction, loop the ribbon or floss on the same side of the outline as in step 1, then go down at D and come up at E (the midpoint of the previous stitch).
3. As the needle is drawn through, the loop of the ribbon or floss will overlap the previous stitch. Continue working in the same direction until the outline is complete.
4. Stem stitches worked in floss and silk ribbon.

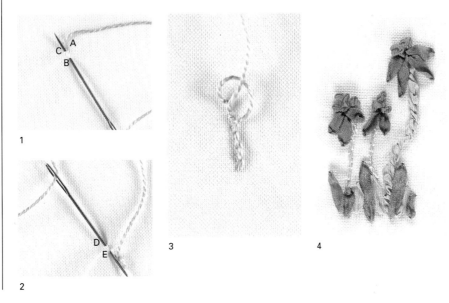

1

2

3

4

LEAF STITCH

The leaf stitch works well with either ribbon or floss. Depending on the width of the stitches, you can make the leaflets long and thin or short and full, and space them widely or densely. The length of an individual frond can also vary, depending on the number of stitches that are used.

1. To make the initial vertical straight stitch, come up at point A and go down at point B. Come back up at C and loop the ribbon below the straight stitch. Insert the needle at D (the same distance from the straight stitch as C, but on the opposite side), and come back up at E, which should be directly below B. Pull the needle and ribbon over the loop.

2. Make a small anchor stitch over the loop to complete the first pair of leaflets.

3. To make a second pair of leaflets (which should be slightly broader than the first pair), come up on the left side at F, then loop the ribbon below the first pair of leaflets and go down at G (the same distance from the central line of anchor stitches as F).

4. Come back up above the center of the loop, then make an anchor stitch to finish the pair of leaflets. Continue adding leaflet pairs by repeating steps 3 and 4, working each successive stitch slightly wider than the one immediately above. Finish a series of leaflets with an anchor stitch.

5. A completed leaf stitch.

6. Leaf stitches stitched with 4mm silk ribbon and embroidery floss, with a Japanese ribbon stitch tulip and French knot buds.

1

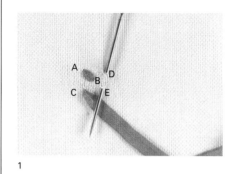

2

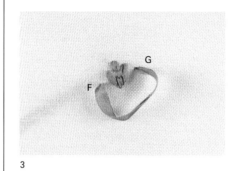

3

4

5

6

WHIP STITCH

If you're inclined to stitch tensely, you'll have to adjust your approach for the whip stitch. Generally used to depict buds and petals, the whip stitch is always worked with a loose, untwisted ribbon. A circular arrangement of curved whip stitches (see steps 4 and 6) is used to make the Bradford rose (see page 49).

1. Make a straight stitch, then come back up alongside point B.
2. Slide the needle underneath the stitch, taking care not to snag the ribbon or pierce the fabric.
3. Keeping the ribbon smooth and flat and using consistent tension, loosely wrap the stitch with the ribbon two or three times.
4. After completing the final wrap, bring the needle through the fabric alongside the center of the wrapped stitch. (By increasing the tension on the ribbon when ending the stitch, the stitch can be curved slightly, producing a curved whip stitch.)
5. A completed whip stitch.
6. Whip stitches and curved whip stitches in 4mm silk ribbon.

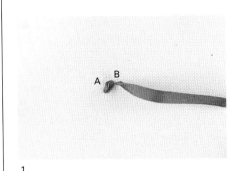

1

2

3

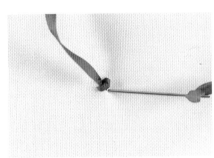

4

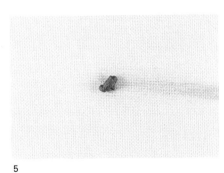

5

6

Knotted Stitches

1. Bring the needle up through the fabric. Holding the ribbon taut, place the needle approximately ⅝ inch from point A.
2. While still holding the ribbon taut, wind it behind the needle.
3. Take the ribbon over the needle, forming one complete wrap.
4. Keeping the wrapped ribbon close to the tip of the needle, place the needle into the fabric very close to point A (but not into it), then gently pull the ribbon through. Hold the knot in place until the stitch is completed.
5. A completed French knot.
6. Groupings of French knots made with 4mm silk and two strands of embroidery floss.

This type of stitch, in which the ribbon or floss is twisted around the needle before both are drawn through the fabric, is commonly used as "filler" to subtly complement or embellish a primary stitch or arrangement of stitches. Among the basic stitches of this group are the French knot and the pistil stitch.

FRENCH KNOT

The French knot is often used as a center for a flower, or several can be arranged in a circle to make a simple forget-me-not. Five to six French knots can be loosely stacked in a cone shape to represent a cluster of grapes or wisteria blossoms, or a cone of knots can be inverted to create hollyhocks.

1

2

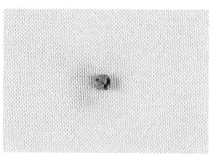

3

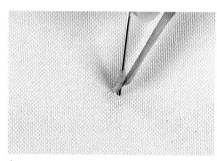

4

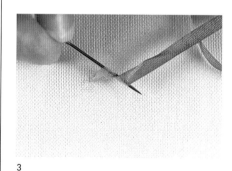

5

6

PISTIL STITCH

The pistil stitch is similar to the French knot, except that the wrapped needle is pulled back through the fabric a short distance away from the point through which it was initially drawn, rather than directly into it. Pistil stitches are frequently used singly in flowers that have conspicuous stamens, such as calla lilies and fuchsias, or grouped to represent tufts of grass.

1. Come up at point A. Wrap the ribbon or floss over the needle two or three times, holding it taut as you wind it.

2. Determine the length of the stitch, then insert needle back into the fabric. Slide the wrapped ribbon or floss down the needle to the surface of the fabric, then slowly pull the needle and floss through.

3. A completed pistil stitch.

4. A trio of pistil stitches illustrating a variety of stitch lengths.

5. Japanese ribbon stitch bluebells stitched in 7mm silk ribbon, with pistil stitch stamens in embroidery floss.

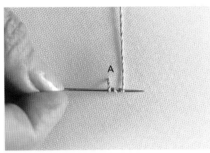

1

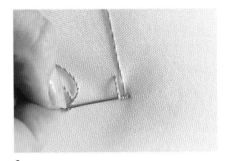

2

3

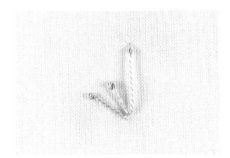

4

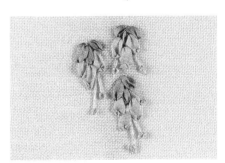

5

Looped Stitches

There are two types of looped stitches. In one group, which includes the lazy daisy, the chain stitch, and the feather stitch, the stitches are formed by passing the needle over a loop of ribbon or floss before it is drawn back through the fabric. In the other are the French knot loop stitch, the loop flower, and the plume stitch, whose stitches are formed by making loops that protrude from the surface of the fabric.

LAZY DAISY

The lazy daisy, which is also referred to as a detached chain stitch (see opposite), is a standard embroidery stitch that lends itself well to silk ribbon embroidery. Note that the length of the lazy daisy's anchor stitch can be varied for a dramatic look.

By adding a straight stitch in a contrasting ribbon within the loop of the lazy daisy (see step 4), you can create a decorative lazy daisy. A decorative lazy daisy can even be worked in three colors—purple for the loop, white for the anchor stitch, and yellow for the straight stitch—to create stunning bearded irises.

1. Bring the needle and ribbon up through the fabric at point A. Keeping the ribbon loose and untwisted, make a loop. Go down at B (immediately adjacent to A) and back up at C so that the needle passes over the ribbon.

2. As the ribbon is pulled through, the loop will tighten.

3. Finish the loop with a small anchor stitch to complete the lazy daisy.

4. To make a decorative lazy daisy, add a straight stitch to the center of the completed lazy daisy using a second color of ribbon.

5. Lazy daisy flowers and leaves stitched in 4mm silk ribbon and embroidery floss.

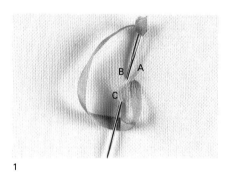

1

2

3

4

5

CHAIN STITCH

A basic embroidery stitch, the chain stitch is comprised of a series of lazy daisies (see opposite). The chain stitch is often used to make stems and vines, or to outline a form.

1. To begin the chain, make a single lazy daisy: Bring the needle and floss up through the fabric at point A, make a loop, then go down at B (immediately adjacent to A) and back up at C so that the needle passes over the floss.

2. Instead of finishing this single lazy daisy with an anchor stitch, loop the floss again, then insert the needle through the fabric at D (immediately adjacent to C) so that passes it *under* the loop of the preceding stitch and emerges at E.

3. The completed second stitch.

4. Repeat step 2 to add "links" to the chain.

5. A completed three-link chain stitch. Finish the last link with a small anchor stitch.

6. Chain stitch stems in 4mm silk ribbon and embroidery floss with lazy daisy flowers.

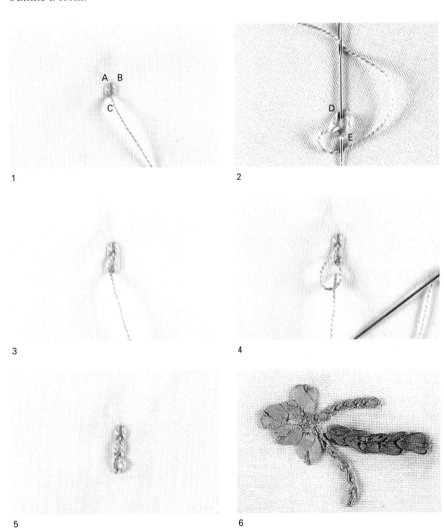

1

2

3

4

5

6

FEATHER STITCH

The feather stitch consists of a series of Y-shaped stitches (individually known as *fly stitches*) alternating from right to left. These stitches can be worked long or short to produce a variety of forms. Feather stitch "stems" can be used to support a single French knot bud or Japanese ribbon stitch petal at each tip, or to depict a sea fan in an aquatic scene.

1. Come up at point A. Working at an angle and curving the ribbon or floss beneath the needle, go down at B and come back up at C.

2. The resulting stitch makes the initial Y shape.

3. Working to the right of the first stitch, go down at D and come back up at E, curving the ribbon or floss beneath the needle.

4. The second Y is formed.

5. Working to the left of the preceding stitch, repeat step 3.

6. The third Y is formed. Add "branches" by continuing to alternate the stitches left and right.

7. A completed feather stitch. Finish the final Y with a small anchor stitch.

8. Feather stitch stems stitched in 4mm silk ribbon and embroidery floss, with French knot crocuses and Japanese ribbon stitch petals and leaves.

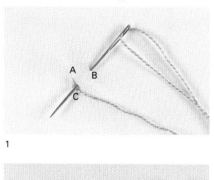

1

2

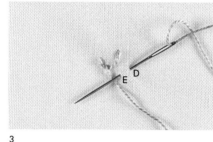

3

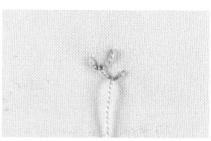

4

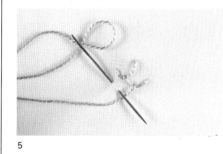

5

6

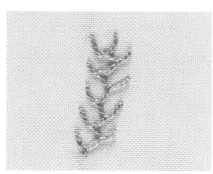

7

8

FRENCH KNOT LOOP STITCH

The French knot loop stitch begins as an incomplete straight stitch. Instead of pulling the ribbon flat against the surface of the fabric, it's left loose to form a little loop, which is then pierced with a French knot. The French knot can be stitched either at the center or at one end of the loop, with either ribbon or floss in the same or a contrasting color (see step 6), or substituted with a bead or pearl. The French knot loop stitch is an easy way to create dimension, and works well as "filler" when stitching a large cluster of flowers.

1. Come up at point A and go down at B (about ⅛ inch from A).

2. Pull the ribbon through the fabric to form a loose loop.

3. Come up through the center of the loop with two strands of floss.

4. Double-wrap the needle with floss to make a French knot in the center of the loop.

5. A completed loop stitch.

6. (From left) French knot loop stitches stitched in 4mm silk ribbon and finished at one end with a ribbon French knot in the same color and width, and in 7mm silk ribbon with French knot centers in floss and 4mm silk ribbon. Also shown: lazy daisy and Japanese ribbon stitch leaves, pistil stitches, and a single French knot.

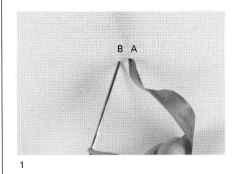

1

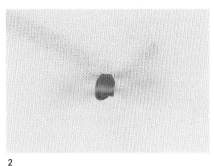

2

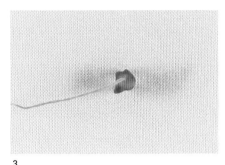

3

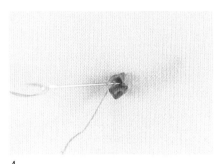

4

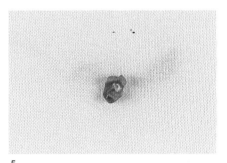

5

6

LOOP FLOWER

This stitch can be a bit of a challenge for a beginner. A single length of ribbon is used to create a flower consisting of four to six loop "petals" arranged around a central point. If too much tension is used to draw the ribbon through the fabric, the preceding loop will be pulled out. You may want to use a laying tool (see page 33) to hold each loop in place while you're stitching the next one. The center of the flower can be finished with a French knot, a bead or pearl, or a straight stitch to secure the final loop to the fabric. The loop flower is not recommended for wearables.

1. Come up at point A and go down at B (about ⅛ inch from A).

2. Use the first loop to plan the position of the remaining petals.

3. Working clockwise around a center point, repeat step 1, taking care not to pull out the preceding loop. If necessary, use a laying tool to hold each loop in place.

4. A completed loop flower with a French knot center.

5. Five-petal loop flowers stitched with 4mm and 7mm silk ribbon, with Japanese ribbon stitch leaves.

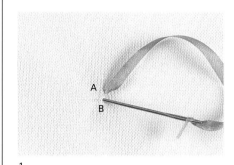

1

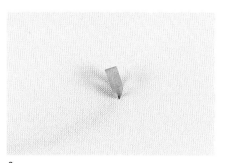

2

3

4

5

PLUME STITCH

The plume stitch is yet another variation on the loop. A series of connecting loops is made by piercing the front of one loop from the back of the fabric to form the next. As with the loop flower, you might need a laying tool to hold each loop in place as you work. A plume stitch can be finished with a straight stitch on the front or back of the fabric (see step 5), or on the front with a single-wrap French knot (see step 6). This stitch is not a good choice for wearables.

1. Come up at point A and go down at B (about 1/8 inch from A).

2. Make a loop approximately 1/4 inch in length.

3. Pierce the front of the preceding loop with the needle. If necessary, hold the loop in place with your thumb or a laying tool.

4. Draw the needle and ribbon through the loop, then go back down through the fabric. Repeat steps 3 and 4 to make additional loops.

5. A completed five-loop plume stitch, finished on the reverse with a straight stitch.

6. Straight, zigzag, and abbreviated plume stitches stitched in 7mm silk ribbon, each finished with a French knot.

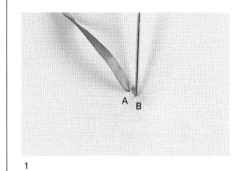

1

2

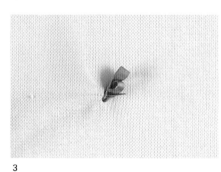

3

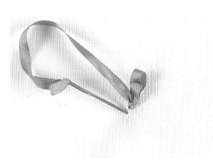

4

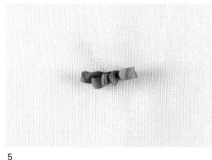

5

6

Roses

It could be argued that the beauty and luster of silk ribbon is best expressed in the voluminous shape of the rose. Silk ribbon embroidery employs several rose stitches, four of which are used in this book. In each case, the rose's circular silhouette and layered form require a gradual build up of stitches. The roses are presented here in order of difficulty, from easiest to most challenging, but this doesn't reflect the stitching time each requires. Note that the spider web rose is the quickest to stitch, followed by the straight stitch rose, with the Bradford rose and the folded rose demanding the longest stitching times.

STRAIGHT STITCH ROSE

The straight stitch rose comprises at least one French knot surrounded by three tiers of overlapping straight stitches. The coloration of the straight stitch rose can be made to look more realistic by using two shades of ribbon in alternate tiers. The circular shape within this rose can also serve as a central cushion for a broad-petaled flower (see step 5). The straight stitch rose works well on wearables, as long as the stitches are short and close to the surface of the fabric.

1. Designate the center of the rose with one large, loosely stitched French knot or three smaller ones. (In this demonstration, a total of three French knots was used.)

2. Encircle the French knots with a tier of slightly overlapping straight stitches. Here, a triangle of straight stitches was used.

3. Add a second tier of overlapping straight stitches that also overlap the first tier slightly. Repeat this step to add a third tier.

4. A completed straight stitch rose.

5. For this 4mm silk ribbon sunflower with Japanese ribbon stitch petals and leaves, the center of a straight stitch rose was modifed to include six French knots and only a single tier of overlapping straight stitches.

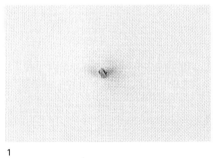
1

2

3

4

5

BRADFORD ROSE

Named for noted Australian stitcher Jenny Bradford, the Bradford rose is composed of at least one French knot surrounded by four whip stitches. To make a larger Bradford rose, begin with more than one French knot, then simply encircle the first tier of whip stitches with a second tier of four or five. (Each subsequent tier must comprise more stitches than the one before it.) Depict the range of shades that can be seen within the layered petals of a real rose by using two shades of silk ribbon for the whip stitches.

1. Determine the center of the rose by stitching a single-wrap French knot. Add a short straight stitch along one side of the knot.
2. Keeping the ribbon flat and working loosely, wrap the straight stitch with two or three passes of the ribbon.
3. Begin a second whip stitch on the other side of French knot, leaving as little space between the two whip stitches as possible. Repeat steps 2 and 3 to complete the tier.
4. A completed single-tier Bradford rose worked with four whip stitches around one French knot.
5. A large Bradford rose consisting of a multiple French knot center stitched with 4mm silk ribbon and two tiers of whip stitches stitched with 7mm silk ribbon. Also shown: Japanese ribbon stitch leaves and French knot buds.

1

2

3

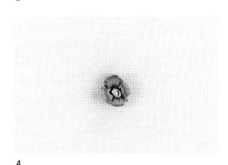

4

5

SPIDER WEB ROSE

A favorite among beginners because it is so easy to execute, the spider web rose is formed by winding the ribbon around an odd number of spokes until they're no longer visible. The underlying framework of the sample stitch shown below is a single feather stitch (more commonly known as a *fly stitch*) that is bolstered with two straight stitches to form a five-spoke wheel.

To enhance the look of your spider web rose, make the first two revolutions with a light shade and the last two with a darker one. As a delightful finishing touch, stitch two or three French knots or add a single seed pearl to the center of a completed rose.

1. Using two strands of floss to match the ribbon, bring the needle through the fabric at point A. Go down at B and come up at C, bringing the tip of the needle over the thread to form a Y shape. Finish the Y by bringing the needle down through the fabric below C so that the stem of the Y is the same length as its diagonals.

2. Make two straight stitches on either side of the Y the same length as the Y's stem and diagonals. Securely knot off the floss on the back of the fabric. (If this foundation is not securely knotted off, the entire rose will fall apart.)

3. Bring the ribbon through the fabric between two spokes and as close to the center as possible.

4. Working in a counterclockwise direction, begin to weave the ribbon under and over the spokes.

5. When the spokes have been wound once, adjust the ribbon to conceal the axis of the spokes.

6. Continue to weave the ribbon over and under the spokes, working loosely and allowing the ribbon to twist and turn.

7. The rose is completed when the spokes are completely hidden by ribbon. Cover the last spoke with ribbon and take the needle down through the fabric, securing the ribbon with a knot on the back of the fabric.

8. Spider web roses with laisy daisy leaves.

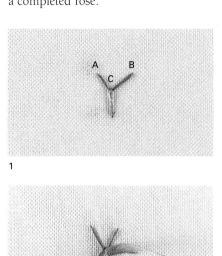

1

2

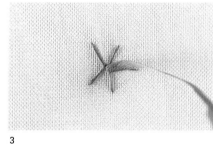

3

4

5

6

7

8

FOLDED ROSE

The folded rose is the perfect marriage of basic ribbon manipulation and silk ribbon embroidery. Due to the ribbon's slippery texture this stitch can be tricky at first, but with practice it can be made quite quickly. (Long fingernails can be a hindrance.) The smallest widths of ribbon that can be used to make this rose are 7mm silk ribbon and 5/8-inch double-sided satin ribbon. For an average-size rose, you'll need about 7 to 9 inches of ribbon. When working with 1- or 1 5/8-inch ribbon you'll need a longer length, depending on the size of the rose you want to make.

1. Tightly roll the ribbon three times.

2. Holding the ribbon roll firmly, secure the layers of the roll by making several small stitches at one end with knotted floss. Leaving the floss attached, proceed to the next step.

3. Holding the roll between thumb and forefinger, fold the top edge of the ribbon back and down.

4. Wrap the folded ribbon once around the center roll to form the first petal.

5. Using the attached floss and needle, secure the first petal by stitching through all the layers at the bottom of the roll.

6. Repeat steps 3 through 5 to make two or three more wraps. Secure each wrap at the bottom of the rose with two tight stitches.

7. After completing the final wrap, trim the excess ribbon to leave a 1/2- to 3/4-inch tail. Bring the needle up through the base of the rose to the center, then back down to the base. Repeat. Finish the base with two stitches, then knot off and cut the floss. Trim the ribbon as close as possible to the base without cutting into the stitching, leaving an 1/8-inch piece of ribbon.

8. Two 7mm silk ribbon folded roses with straight stitch buds and Japanese ribbon stitch and lazy daisy leaves in 4mm ribbon. Roses are attached to fabric with several small stitches using floss and an embroidery needle.

1

2

3

4

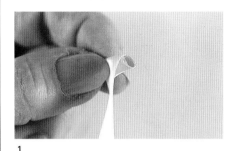

5

6

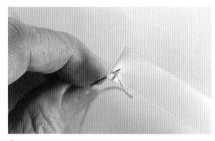

7

8

Accessories

Accessories add special finishing touches to your wardrobe's every season and mood. The simple designs featured in this chapter are guaranteed not to overwhelm the objects, the person who wears or uses them, or, most important, the stitcher who embellishes them. Moreover, the relatively small scale of most personal accessories can make the prospect of stitching an entire project far less intimidating, especially for a beginner. Each project in this chapter offers a distinct set of challenges designed to develop ribbon embroidery skills.

Linen Handkerchief

SKILL LEVEL
Beginner

TIME TO COMPLETE
1 hour

STITCHES USED
Loop flower
Padded straight stitch
French knot
Lazy daisy
Stem stitch
Pistil stitch
Straight stitch

SUPPLIES
Project
Purchased celery green linen handkerchief

Stitch Pattern
Page 119

Silk Ribbon
1 yard 4mm burgundy
1 yard 4mm mauve
16 inches 4mm ivory

Thread or Floss
1 skein variegated light green rayon thread (worked with one strand) OR 1 skein light green embroidery floss (worked with two strands)

1 skein variegated mauve rayon thread (worked with one strand) OR 1 skein mauve embroidery floss (worked with two strands)

Miscellaneous
Water-soluble marking pen
4-inch hoop

Reflecting the recent resurgence of interest in Victorian design, embellished handkerchiefs are making something of a comeback. The handkerchief that serves as the setting for the simple design on page 119 was chosen from my collection of vintage handkerchiefs. You can find inexpensive and attractive handkerchiefs in many antique and vintage clothing stores. I picked up on the subtle coloration of my piece's edging by using variegated thread to stitch a few of the design elements. The linen fabric and loosely crocheted variegated green edging make this handkerchief a candidate for handwashing in lukewarm water and a mild detergent.

The versatile stitch design is visually pleasing regardless of its orientation. It would also work well on an eyeglass case or a lingerie bag, or as an accent on an infant's garment or a blouse collar or pocket flap. Although loop flowers are generally considered too delicate for most wearables and accessories, the straight stitches used to tack down their petals make them more durable.

TRANSFER METHOD
Centering the design in one corner of the handkerchief, use the water-soluble marking pen to mark the centers of the loop flowers and to lightly sketch in the stem stitch lines.

STITCHING INSTRUCTIONS
1. Stitch the lower right-hand loop flower with burgundy silk ribbon.
2. Stitch the upper left-hand loop flower with mauve silk ribbon.
3. Stitch the left-hand loop flower's padded straight stitch bud with mauve silk ribbon.
4. Stitch three French knots with mauve ribbon in the center of the burgundy loop flower.
5. Stitch three French knots with burgundy silk ribbon in the center of the mauve loop flower.
6. Stitch the burgundy loop flower's padded straight stitch buds with burgundy silk ribbon.
7. Stitch three lazy daisy leaves among the loop flowers' petals with ivory silk ribbon.
8. Stitch the stem stitches and lazy daisy leaves in green thread or floss.
9. Stitch the pistil stitches in mauve thread or floss.
10. To secure the petals of the loop flowers to the fabric, use mauve thread or floss to add a tiny straight stitch through each loop. Bring the needle and thread up through the fabric near the wide end of the loop and as close to the silk as possible. Pass the needle through the loop, then pull it back through the fabric as close as possible to the other edge of the ribbon.

(Right) The completed handkerchief, with a detail showing how the colors of the crocheted fringe were repeated in the ivory silk ribbon and the variegated green thread (below right).

Battenberg Lace Eyeglass Case

SKILL LEVEL
Beginner

TIME TO COMPLETE
1 hour

STITCHES USED
Spider web rose
French knot
Japanese ribbon stitch

SUPPLIES
Project
Purchased white
Battenberg lace eyeglass
case

Stitch Pattern
Page 119

Silk Ribbon
20 inches 7mm purple
16 inches 7mm terracotta
16 inches 7mm light
purple
16 inches 7mm peach
16 inches 7mm light
forest green

Embroidery Floss
Worked with two strands
1 skein pale peach
1 skein white

Embellishments
3 8mm frosted lavender
beads
4 8mm iridescent glass
beads
7 lavender bugle beads
7 turquoise glass seed
beads

Miscellaneous
Water-soluble marking pen
4-inch hoop (optional)

Because the eyeglass case in this project was purchased already made, its design had to be stitched close to the top of the case and without a hoop. With this in mind, I devised a compact cluster of spider web roses, French knots, and delicate beads to accent the closure. Although Battenberg lace is woven from broad strips of cotton, the decorative pattern of the openwork won't interfere with your stitching.

If you're planning to make your own eyeglass case from a pattern, choose muslin, broadcloth, or cotton for the foundation fabric, and purchase enough fabric and lace so that they can both be stretched on a 4-inch hoop. After the stitching is complete, cut the fabric and the lace to the pattern, then sew and assemble the case as directed.

This design can also be applied to the pocket flaps on a blouse, or at the center point of a camisole's neckline.

TRANSFER METHOD
Use the water-soluble marking pen to mark the centers of the spider web roses.

STITCHING INSTRUCTIONS
1. Using the pale peach embroidery floss to create the foundation spokes for each flower, stitch the center spider web rose with terracotta silk ribbon, the left-hand rose with light purple silk ribbon, and the right-hand rose with peach silk ribbon.
2. Loosely stitch the Y shape of single-wrap French knots with purple silk ribbon.
3. Stitch the Japanese ribbon stitch leaves with light forest green silk ribbon.
4. Using a #10 beading needle and white embroidery floss, stitch one frosted lavender bead into the center of each rose.
5. Add one iridescent bead on either side of the point where the diagonals of the French knot Y meet its stem, and in the space between each side rose and the Japanese ribbon stitch leaves.
6. Surround the stem of the Y with a semi-oval of bugle beads.
7. Complete the design by adding a turquoise seed bead beneath each bugle bead.

(Right) The complete eyeglass case, and a detail showing the relationship between stitches and embellishments (opposite).

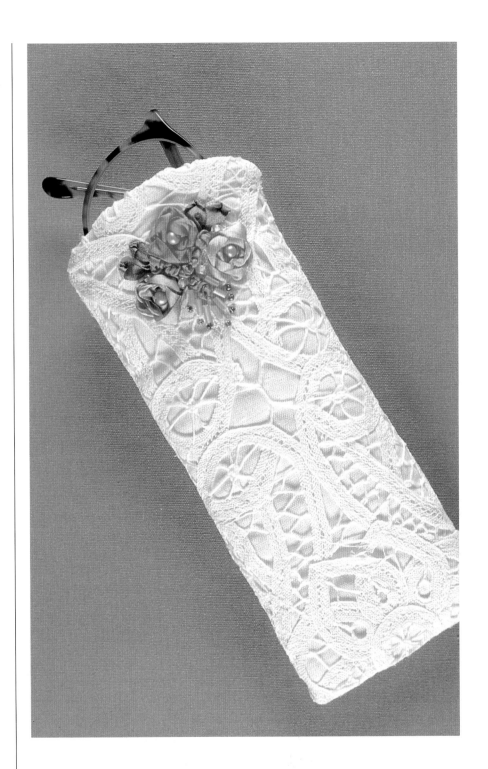

Fringed Silk Purse

SKILL LEVEL
Intermediate

TIME TO COMPLETE
4 hours

STITCHES USED
Twisted Japanese ribbon stitch

Loop flower

SUPPLIES

Project

Purchased terracotta Dupionni silk purse with fringe

Stitch Pattern

Page 119

Silk Ribbon

1½ yards 4mm variegated mauve

1½ yards 4mm variegated purple

1 yard 4mm mauve

1 yard 4mm purple ribbon

Synthetic Ribbon

½ yard green Mokuba Raysheen Tape OR ½ yard 7mm green silk ribbon

Thread and Floss

1 skein green embroidery floss (worked with one strand)

1 spool gold metallic thread

Embellishments

32 metallic green, burgundy, and gray glass seed beads

Miscellaneous

Water-soluble marking pen

Although the curling, spiraling stitches and two shades of variegated silk ribbon heighten the elaborate appearance of this design, it actually consists of just two stitches: the twisted Japanese ribbon stitch and the loop flower. The petals of the loop flowers are stitched randomly rather than in the customary circular pattern, creating a crowded mass that hides the starting points of the Japanese ribbon stitches.

The purse featured in this project is made from Dupionni silk (also known as Dupion, Duppioni, or Douppioni silk; from *doppione,* Italian for "double" or "duplicate"). This fabric is made from silk reeled from two cocoons that are slightly enmeshed because they were spun side by side. This silk filament creates a thread with pronounced but irregular *slubbing,* or twisting, that is also evident in the softly lustrous fabrics it is used to weave. The design can be stitched on any flap-closure handbag made from a lightweight fabric.

As the stitching surface is small and the stitch forms are comparatively large, a hoop is not recommend for this project.

TRANSFER METHOD
Use the water-soluble marking pen to mark the center of each spider mum.

STITCHING INSTRUCTIONS

1. Using mauve and variegated mauve silk ribbons, stitch the twisted Japanese ribbon stitch petals in a circle around the center of each flower, leaving enough room for the loop flowers (see step 2). Twist each stitch three times and make each one a slightly different length.
2. Stitch a six-petal loop flower in the center of each circle of Japanese ribbon stitches with the purple and variegated purple silk ribbons. (Add as many loops as necessary to fill the circle completely.)
3. Using a #18 chenille needle, stitch the twisted Japanese ribbon stitch leaves with raysheen tape, twisting the tape only once. Instead of dragging the tape from one stitch to the next, finish each stitch with a ¼-inch tail, then tack the stitch down on the reverse with three small straight stitches in matching floss. (Note that the tape is too thick to begin the stitch with a soft knot.)
4. Using gold thread and a #10 beading needle, randomly stitch all of the beads among the three spider mums.

(Above) The completed purse, with a detail showing the relationship of the central loop flowers and the twisted Japanese ribbon stitches (right).

Velvet Beret

SKILL LEVEL
Intermediate

TIME TO COMPLETE
6 hours

STITCHES USED
Lazy daisy
Japanese ribbon stitch
French knot
Leaf stitch
Stem stitch
Feather stitch

SUPPLIES

Project
Purchased navy velvet
beret

Stitch Pattern
Page 120

Silk Ribbon
7mm Width
½ yard terracotta
½ yard dark olive green
½ yard bright yellow

4mm Width
2 yards terracotta
2 yards pale pink
2 yards light peach
1½ yards ivory
1½ yards teal
1½ yards peach
1 yard dark teal
1 yard celery green
1 yard light blue
1 yard dark olive green
½ yard purple

Thread or Floss
1 card celery green silk
buttonhole twist *OR* 1
skein celery green
embroidery floss (worked
with two strands)
1 skein ecru embroidery
floss

Embellishments
11 4mm pearls
9 8mm pearls

Miscellaneous
White or yellow fabric
pencil
Fabric eraser

Impressed with its classic look, I purchased the vintage beret shown opposite in an antique store. Made of a high-quality cotton navy velvet and lined with navy grosgrain, its beautifully constructed shape offered a sumptuous background for an array of basic stitches. Purchase a velvet beret made of a natural-fiber fabric (cotton or silk); the additional expense will be money well spent. Synthetic velvets are heavier, bulkier, and require more effort to manipulate while stitching. (The stitch pattern would also work well on a traditional flat wool beret.) In addition to the fact that my beret's complex, eight-gored construction immediately ruled out working with a hoop, I didn't want to risk destroying the velvet's beautiful nap with ugly hoop marks.

TRANSFER METHOD

Use a sharpened white or yellow fabric pencil to mark the centers of the lazy daisy and Japanese ribbon stitch flowers. After stitching the flowers, lightly trace the lines for the stem and feather stitches. Once the stitching is complete, remove any visible sketch marks with the fabric eraser and a damp cloth.

STITCHING INSTRUCTIONS

1. Starting with the central grouping of lazy daisy flowers and working from left to right, stitch one each of the flowers using 4mm silk ribbon in the following colors: purple, dark teal, terracotta, peach, light blue, and pale pink.
2. Stitch the large Japanese ribbon stitch flower with 7mm terracotta ribbon.
3. Stitch the two arcs of Japanese ribbon stitches next to the purple and dark teal lazy daisy flowers with peach silk ribbon.
4. Add a French knot with pale pink silk ribbon beneath each of the Japanese ribbon stitches.
5. Stitch the leaf stitch above and to the right of the pale pink lazy daisy flower with 4mm celery green silk ribbon.
6. Stitch the leaf stitch to the immediate right of the pale pink lazy daisy flower with 4mm dark olive green silk ribbon.
7. Using purple and pale pink silk ribbons, stitch the two clusters of single-wrap French knots above the peach and pale pink lazy daisy flowers.
8. Stitch the two sets of French knot clusters below the purple lazy daisy flower with 4mm light blue, ivory, teal, dark teal, terracotta, and peach silk ribbons.
9. Stitch the Japanese ribbon stitch leaves adjacent to the lazy daisy flowers and French knot clusters and along the bottom of the stem stitches with 7mm dark olive silk ribbon.
10. Stitch the stem and feather stitches with celery green silk buttonhole twist.
11. Stitch the lazy daisy leaves that run along the top of the stem stitches with 4mm celery green silk ribbon.
12. Stitch the Japanese ribbon stitch buds among the feather stitches with 7mm bright yellow silk ribbon.
13. Use ivory silk ribbon to stitch single-wrap French knots at the tips of the feather stitches.
14. Using a #10 beading needle, stitch one 8mm pearl in center of each lazy daisy flower.
15. Randomly stitch the 4mm pearls among the French knot silk ribbon clusters.

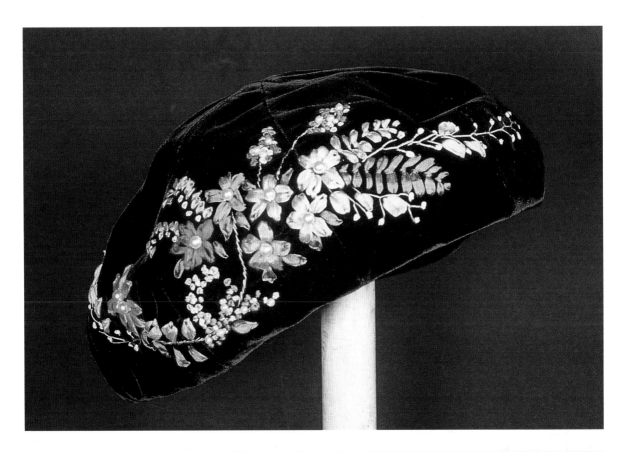

(Above) The completed beret, with a detail of the central arrangement of lazy daisy flowers with 8mm pearl centers (right).

Silk Evening Bag

SKILL LEVEL
Intermediate

TIME TO COMPLETE
16 hours

STITCHES USED
Stem stitch
Padded straight stitch
French knot

SUPPLIES
Project
Purchased black Dupionni
silk evening bag

Stitch Pattern
Page 121

Silk Ribbon
2 yards 4mm bright
yellow
2 yards 4mm ivory
1 yard 4mm light olive
green
1 yard 4mm forest green

Thread and Floss
1 skein forest green
embroidery floss (worked
with two strands)
1 spool gold metallic
thread

Embellishments
Antique-finish gold glass
seed beads
Antique-finish copper
glass seed beads

Miscellaneous
White marking pencil
Fabric eraser
4-inch hoop

In contrast to the other purse project in this chapter (see pages 58–59), the stitch design of this elegant evening bag, an adaptation of a mid-19th century piece of English embroidery, is deceptively simple. Although only three stitches are used, the scope and detail of the design make it somewhat time-consuming to stitch.

The size and shape of this purse permitted the use of a 4-inch hoop. To minimize creasing, insert one stave inside the bag.

TRANSFER METHOD

Use a white marking pencil to lightly sketch the bouquet of flowers in the center of the purse front. When the stitching for that part of the design has been completed, remove the hoop and lightly sketch the surrounding vine, which should follow the outline of the purse shape. After all the stitching is complete, remove any visible marks with the fabric eraser and a damp cloth.

STITCHING INSTRUCTIONS

1. Stitch the stems of the central bouquet of flowers with forest green floss.
2. Stitch the padded straight stitch buds with bright yellow and ivory silk ribbons and the leaves with light olive green silk ribbon.
3. After sketching in the surrounding vine, stitch the stem stitches with forest green floss.
4. Stitch the padded straight stitch buds and the five-petal padded straight stitch flowers with bright yellow and ivory silk ribbons, and the leaves with light olive green and forest green silk ribbons.
5. Use bright yellow or ivory silk ribbon to add a single-wrap French knot to the center of each five-petal flower.
6. Using a #10 beading needle and the gold metallic thread, randomly stitch the beads among the flowers and leaves on both sides of the vine.

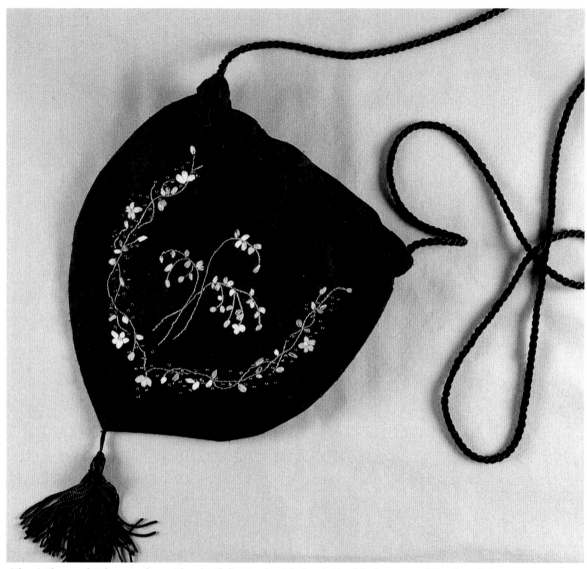

(Above) The completed evening bag, with a detail showing the right-hand side of the bouquet and vine (opposite).

Wearables

What better way to advertise your stitching skills than to wear them? And what could be more gratifying than to receive compliments on your ribbon artistry? The crafter's term "wearable" is short for "wearable art." This chapter contains seven easy projects—two for children, five for adults—all of which are stitched on classic garments. The results are guaranteed to elicit admiration from onlookers.

Infant Cuff Cap and Mittens

SKILL LEVEL
Beginner

TIME TO COMPLETE
1½ hours

STITCHES USED
Japanese ribbon stitch
Lazy daisy
French knot

SUPPLIES
Project
Purchased infant or
toddler cuff cap and
matching mittens

Stitch Patterns
Page 121

Silk Ribbon
1½ yards 7mm pink
1 yard 7mm lavender
1 yard 4mm light green
1 yard 4mm lemon yellow
16 inches 7mm blue

Miscellaneous
Water-soluble marking pen

This project offers the beginning stitcher a simple exercise in working with 7mm ribbons. To accommodate the width of the ribbon and to prevent snagging the loose weave of the knitted fabric, use a tapestry needle, which has a large eye and a blunt point.

TRANSFER METHOD

Use the water-soluble marking pen to mark the centers of the Japanese ribbon stitch flowers on both the cuff cap and the mittens.

STITCHING INSTRUCTIONS

Although I chose to stitch the design only on the folded cuff, you might prefer to give the stitches a little added stability by drawing the needle and ribbon through the cuff and the portion of the cap immediately below it.

CUFF CAP

1. Stitch the Japanese ribbon stitch flower in the center of the design with 7mm pink silk ribbon.
2. Working the design from left to right, stitch the four remaining Japanese ribbon stitch flowers with 7mm silk ribbon: two in lavender, one in light blue, and one in pink.
3. Stitch the lazy daisy leaves with 4mm light green silk ribbon.
4. Stitch the French knot centers of the Japanese ribbon stitch flowers with 4mm lemon yellow silk ribbon.

MITTENS

Stitch one mitten at a time. The completed mitten can then serve as a model for the second.

1. Stitch the Japanese ribbon stitch flowers with 7mm pink silk ribbon. If necessary, make the petals slightly smaller than those on the cap so that the flower fits the mitten cuffs.
2. Stitch the lazy daisy leaves with 4mm green silk ribbon.
3. Stitch the French knot center of the flower with 4mm yellow silk ribbon.

(Above) The complete cap and mittens, with a detail of the center trio of Japanese ribbon stitch flowers with French knot centers and lazy daisy leaves (opposite).

Toddler "Bubble" Ensemble

SKILL LEVEL
Beginner

TIME TO COMPLETE
6 hours (for the entire set)

STITCHES USED
French knot
Japanese ribbon stitch
Lazy daisy

SUPPLIES
Project
Purchased one-piece
cotton toddler "bubble"
suit with large white
collar, ballet slippers, and
bonnet

Stitch Patterns
Page 122

Silk Ribbon
2 1/2 yards 4mm coral
2 yards 4mm pale yellow
2 yards 4mm deep rose
2 yards 4mm lilac
I yard 4mm light teal
1 yard 4mm celery green

Embroidery Floss
1 skein celery green floss
(worked with two strands)

Embellishments
1 yard 5/8-inch double-
sided pink satin ribbon (to
match the ribbon on the
bonnet)

Miscellaneous
Water-soluble marking pen
Tracing paper
Black fineline marker
Tulle netting
Fray Check

A standard body shape in infant and toddler apparel, the bubble suit (also widely known as a romper) is easy to find in many children's clothing stores. Embellished with a simple arrangement of Japanese ribbon stitch flowers that is repeated on a lacy bonnet and ballet slippers, this bubble suit with portrait collar would transform any little girl into a vision of springtime. The stitches all lay flat against the surface of the fabric, so they can more readily withstand frequent wear and laundering. The simplicity of the stitches and the small size of the stitching surfaces make working with a hoop unnecessary.

TRANSFER METHOD
Use the water-soluble marking pen to mark the suit, bonnet, and slippers with the centers of the Japanese ribbon stitch flowers. To adjust the orientation of the pattern for the right-hand collar so that it conforms to the curve of the left-hand collar, trace the design on tracing paper with a black fineline marker. Turn the traced design face down, then trace it on tulle netting with the black marker. Pin the netting to the collar and trace the design on the fabric with a water-soluble pen.

STITCHING INSTRUCTIONS
Stitch the patterns in the following sequence: the two sides of the collar, the two pockets, the bonnet, then the slippers.
1. Stitch the single-wrap French knot centers for the Japanese ribbon stitch flowers with assorted colors of silk ribbon.
2. Using one color for each flower, stitch the Japanese ribbon stitch flowers with assorted colors of silk ribbon.
3. Stitch the small lazy daisy leaves with celery green floss.
4. Stitch the large lazy daisy leaves with celery green silk ribbon.
5. Cut three 8-inch lengths from the satin ribbon. Tie each length in a bow.
6. Attach one bow to the center of the suit collar with a safety pin.
7. Stitch each of the remaining two bows to the center of the elastic strap on each slipper.
8. Coat the ends of the stitches on the reverse of the fabric and the ends of the bows on the slippers with Fray Check. After the Fray Check has dried, trim the ends of the bows to sharp angles.

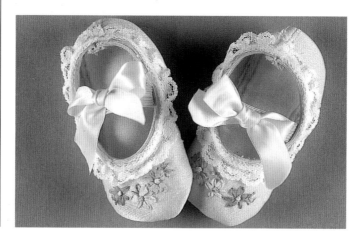

(Opposite) The completed bubble suit, bonnet, and ballet slippers, with a detail of the ballet slippers (left).

Linen Blouse

SKILL LEVEL
Beginner

TIME TO COMPLETE
4 hours

STITCHES USED
Japanese ribbon stitch
French knot
Leaf stitch
Stem stitch
Lazy daisy
Pistil stitch

SUPPLIES

Project
Purchased yellow linen blouse with round neckline

Stitch Patterns
Page 123

Silk Ribbon
2 1/2 yards 4mm celery green
2 yards 4mm pink
1 1/2 yards 4mm blue
1 yard 4mm bronze
1 yard 4mm dark green
1 yard 4mm terracotta
1 yard 4mm lavender

Embroidery Floss
1 skein celery green
(worked with three strands)

Miscellaneous
Tracing paper
Permanent black fineline marker
Tulle netting
Water-soluble marking pen

Having survived several seasons and frequent handwashings, the blouse featured in this project stands as a testament to the durability of silk ribbon embellishment. Because I sometimes wear the blouse while teaching silk ribbon embroidery classes, students have asked me to sketch the design for them so that they can stitch it at home. The design can be applied to any blouse with a round, collarless neckline, and the delicate palette of silk ribbon would enhance nearly every background color.

Since linen wrinkles easily, I decided to stitch this project without a hoop to make the task of ironing the garment afterward less difficult. I used the tulle netting transfer method to avoid rubbing and pulling on the weave of the linen while trying to erase transfer marks.

TRANSFER METHOD
Using the tulle netting transfer method (see page 24), lightly trace the design on the blouse with the water-soluble marking pen.

STITCHING INSTRUCTIONS
Stitch one side of the neckline first, then the other.
1. Stitch the five-petal Japanese ribbon stitch flowers with blue silk ribbon.
2. Stitch a single-wrap French knot in the center of each flower with bronze silk ribbon.
3. Stitch the leaf stitches with dark green silk ribbon.
4. Stitch the stem stitch stems and vines with celery green floss.
5. Stitch the lazy daisy leaves with celery green silk ribbon.
6. Stitch the three-petal Japanese ribbon stitch hanging flowers with terracotta and pink silk ribbons.
7. Stitch the clusters of single-wrap French knots with lavender and peach silk ribbons.
8. Stitch the pistil stitch accents with celery green floss.

(Above) The completed
blouse, with a detail of
the right yoke (right).

Silken Camisole and Tap Pant

SKILL LEVEL
Beginner

TIME TO COMPLETE
6 hours

STITCHES USED
Spider web rose
Lazy daisy
French knot
Feather stitch
Straight stitch

SUPPLIES
Project
Purchased ivory polyester
camisole and tap pant
Stitch Patterns
Page 124
Silk Ribbon
3½ yards 4mm mauve
3 yards 4mm lavender
2 yards 4mm pale yellow
24 inches 4mm celery
green
Embroidery Floss
1 skein mauve (worked
with two strands)
1 skein celery green
(worked with two strands)
Miscellaneous
Water-soluble marking pen

The elegant designs in this project can easily be stitched by a beginner. The finished camisole set would be an excellent gift for a bride—and she'd never guess that you could stitch the project in one day. The set pictured is 100-percent polyester, which has the glossy look and feel of silk but is much easier to stitch and launder. Since there is no possibility of shrinkage or fading, this garment doesn't need to be laundered in preparation for stitching. The placement of the stitches and the cut of the garment excludes the use of a hoop.

By adjusting the color scheme, these designs could also work on the corner of a handkerchief, on the four corners of a breadbasket cover, or as a central motif on a baby's one-piece suit.

TRANSFER METHOD
Use the water-soluble marking pen to mark the centers of the spider web roses and the lazy daisy flowers. After the stitching is complete, remove any visible markings with a damp cloth.

STITCHING INSTRUCTIONS
1. Working on one side of the camisole only, stitch the spider web roses with mauve silk ribbon. Use mauve embroidery floss to create the foundation spokes for each flower.
2. Stitch the single lazy daisy rosebuds with mauve silk ribbon.
3. Stitch the five-petal lazy daisy flowers with lavender silk ribbon.
4. Stitch the French knots with pale yellow silk ribbon. Work the centers of the lavender lazy daisy flowers with less tension so that they are slightly larger than the French knots surrounding the spider web rose.
5. Stitch the lazy daisy leaves with celery green silk ribbon.
6. Stitch the feather stitches with celery green embroidery floss.
7. At the tip of each feather stitch, stitch a double-wrap French knot with mauve floss.
8. Repeat steps 1 through 7, first on the other side of the camisole, then on each of the two legs of the tap pant. On the tap pant, add small straight stitch stamens to the anchor stitches of the mauve silk ribbon lazy daisy rosebuds.

(Above) The completed set, with details for the camisole (right) and tap pant (opposite).

Cotton Chambray Jumper

SKILL LEVEL
Beginner

TIME TO COMPLETE
7 hours

STITCHES USED
Lazy daisy
Leaf stitch
Stem stitch
Japanese ribbon stitch
French knot
Pistil stitch
Bradford rose

SUPPLIES

Project
Purchased chambray
jumper

Stitch Patterns
Pages 124 and 125

Silk Ribbon
4½ yards 4mm olive
green

3 yards 4mm lilac

1½ yards 4mm gold

1½ yards 4mm lime
green

1 yard 4mm hot pink

1 yard 4mm purple

1 yard 4mm light purple

1 yard 4mm ivory

Embroidery Floss
1 skein dark green
(worked with three
strands)

Miscellaneous
Tracing paper
Permanent black fineline
marker
Tulle netting
Water-soluble marking pen
4-inch hoop

The larger scale and narrow, tapered shoulders of the jumper in this project invite a more expansive, flowing embroidery design than any of the preceding projects. All of the motifs in this design, including the French knot wisteria blossoms and the sinuous stem stitch vines, emphasize the cascade of silk ribbon.

Cotton chambray is available in three colors—blue, black, and red—and in a single weight similar to that of the cotton fabric used to make bed linens. A chambray's *warp*, or vertical threads, are always colored, while its *weft*, or horizontal threads, are always white. Blue chambray is often mistaken for denim, a much heavier and stiffer fabric. To keep the fabric taut during stitching, work this project with a 4-inch hoop.

TRANSFER METHOD

Using the tulle netting transfer method (see page 24), lightly trace the designs on the jumper with the water-soluble marking pen. After the stitching is complete, remove any visible marks with a damp cotton swab.

STITCHING INSTRUCTIONS

DESIGN 1: RIGHT SHOULDER
1. Stitch the six-petal lazy daisy flowers with hot pink silk ribbon.
2. Stitch the five-petal lazy daisy flowers with gold silk ribbon.
3. Stitch the leaf stitches with lime green silk ribbon.
4. Except for the hanging floral vines, stitch the stem stitch stems and vines with dark green floss.
5. Stitch the lazy daisy leaves with olive green silk ribbon.
6. Stitch the Japanese ribbon stitch hanging flowers with light purple silk ribbon.
7. Stitch the segments of vine between the hanging flowers with dark green floss.
8. Stitch the pistil stitch stamens that hang from the last flower on the vine.
9. Stitch the French knot clusters with lilac and light purple silk ribbons.
10. Stitch a single-wrap French knot in the center of each lazy daisy flower. Use purple silk ribbon for the gold flowers, and gold silk ribbon for the hot pink flowers.
11. Stitch one Bradford rose each with light purple and purple silk ribbons.

DESIGN 2: LEFT SHOULDER
1. Stitch the five-petal lazy daisy flowers with hot pink silk ribbon.
2. Stitch the leaf stitches with lime green silk ribbon.
3. Except for the hanging floral vines, stitch the stem stitch stems and vines with dark green floss.
4. Stitch the lazy daisy leaves with olive green silk ribbon.
5. Stitch the Japanese ribbon stitch hanging flowers with light purple and lilac silk ribbons.
6. Stitch the segments of vine between the hanging flowers with dark green floss.
7. Stitch five double-wrap French knots that run along the bottom of the longest tendril with olive green silk ribbon.
8. Stitch the pistil stitch stamens that hang from each of the last flowers on the vine.
9. Stitch the French knot clusters with gold and ivory silk ribbons.
10. Stitch a single-wrap French knot in the center of each lazy daisy flower with gold silk ribbon.

(Above) The completed jumper, with a detail of the right shoulder (right).

Damask Waistcoat

SKILL LEVEL
Beginner

TIME TO COMPLETE
8 hours

STITCHES USED
Stem stitch
Spider web rose
Padded straight stitch
French knot loop stitch
French knot
Japanese ribbon stitch
Pistil stitch
Straight stitch

SUPPLIES
Project
Purchased waistcoat
Stitch Patterns
Pages 126–128
Silk Ribbon
6 yards 4mm pale grass
green
3 yards 4mm dusty rose
1¹/₂ yards 4mm pink
1 yard 7mm pink
Embroidery Floss
1 skein pale grass green
floss (worked with two
strands)
1 skein pink floss (worked
with two strands)
1 skein ecru floss (worked
with two strands)
Embellishments
17 4mm pearls
5 9mm pearls
3 antique pearl buttons
Miscellaneous
Tracing paper
Permanent black fineline
marker
Tulle netting
Water-soluble marking pen
4-inch hoop

During a recent trip to Paris, I was inspired by the vests and waistcoats (pronounced WES-kits) that many of the French women were wearing, and wanted to design a vest-style blouse that could be worn formally with a long black velvet skirt or trousers. I wanted the stitch design to begin at the vest points and run around the neckline and down the front of the blouse. After much searching, I couldn't find a ready-made version, so I had the waistcoat featured in this project sewn from a basic vest pattern out of ivory Puenchken damask and lined with satin. (The term *Puenchken* is German for "tooled" or "embossed," referring to the raised diamond pattern in the fabric.)

Damask is usually woven from a blend of 55 percent cotton and 45 percent rayon, which gives it its elegant luster. It can be handwashed or machine-washed on the delicate cycle with a low-suds detergent, then air-dried. Dry cleaning is recommended only if the stitching won't be distorted by the pressing equipment.

TRANSFER METHOD

Using the tulle netting transfer method (see page 24), lightly trace the designs on the blouse with the water-soluble marking pen. After the stitching is complete, remove any visible marks with a damp cotton swab.

STITCHING INSTRUCTIONS

This project is worked most efficiently one *stitch* at a time, rather than one *design* at a time.

1. Using pale green floss, stitch the stem stitch stems and vines.
2. Stitch the spider web roses with the dusty rose and pink silk ribbons, using the pink floss to create foundation spokes for each flower.
3. Stitch the padded straight stitch buds with dusty rose silk ribbon.
4. Stitch the French knot loop flowers stitch with pink silk ribbon.
5. Stitch the French knot clusters with pink and dusty rose silk ribbons.
6. Stitch the Japanese ribbon stitch leaves with pale green silk ribbon.
7. Stitch the pistil stitch with pink or pale green floss.
8. Add small straight stitch stamens to the padded straight stitch buds.
9. Using ecru floss, stitch a 4mm pearl in the center of each spider web rose, then stitch the remaining pearls throughout the rest of the design.
10. Use ecru floss to add the pearl buttons. (Make sure that the buttons fit the buttonholes.)

(Above) The completed waistcoat, with a detail of the back neckline (opposite) and one of the designs between the buttons (right).

Brocade Vest

SKILL LEVEL
Intermediate

TIME TO COMPLETE
20 hours

STITCHES USED
Japanese ribbon stitch
Lazy daisy
Twisted Japanese ribbon stitch
Leaf stitch
Stem stitch
French knot
Feather stitch

SUPPLIES
Project
Black brocade vest with lapels and pocket flaps

Stitch Patterns
Pages 129 and 130

Silk Ribbon
7mm Width
1½ yards light orange
40 inches light purple
1 yard purple
28 inches dark teal
16 inches orange
16 inches light teal
16 inches pink
16 inches ivory
10 inches lilac
8 inches coral
4mm Width
4 yards purple
2 yards lilac
2 yards grass green
2 yards light green
2 yards white
1 yard pink
16 inches yellow
16 inches lime green

(supply list continued on page 80)

I sewed this simple men's-style vest from two yards of black silk brocade I found in an antique store, though any purchased vest, jacket, or coat with lapels and pocket flaps can work with these patterns. Brocades, which are also referred to as tapestries or jacquards, are characterized by raised patterns that are woven into the cloth. Stitching with silk ribbon on brocade is no different from stitching on a plain fabric ground. The floral pattern within the fabric served as the inspiration for the embroidery designs, and the black background provided a vivid contrast for the bright colors of the silk ribbon. (In addition, black is particularly versatile, as it can be worn for both casual and formal occasions.) If you're stitching on ivory or white brocade, use pale pastels and mauves; bright primary colors work well on blue denim. Since the lapels can be stitched with up to four distinct designs, use only the patterns that best suit the proportions of your purchased or hand-sewn item.

TRANSFER METHOD
Use the white fabric pencil to lightly mark the principal elements of each design. Mark any or all of the following as needed:
- The centers of the Japanese ribbon stitch flowers
- The center lines of the feather stitches
- The lines of the stem stitches

   After the stitching is complete, remove any visible pencil marks with the fabric eraser.

STITCHING INSTRUCTIONS
The order in which you stitch the designs should reflect the number of large flowers each contains. Start with the design that has the most flowers, then work designs with successively fewer flowers.

DESIGN 1: UPPER LEFT LAPEL
1. Stitch one Japanese ribbon stitch flower each in 7mm orange, light orange, light teal, pink, and ivory silk ribbons.
2. Stitch the lazy daisy leaves with 4mm lime green silk ribbon.
3. Stitch the leaf stitches with 4mm grass green silk ribbon.
4. Stitch the stem stitches with green embroidery floss.
5. Using 4mm light green silk ribbon, stitch Japanese ribbon stitch leaves on either side of each stem.
6. Stitch the feather stitches with green silk buttonhole twist.
7. Add French knots in 4mm white silk ribbon to the tips of the feather stitches.
8. Stitch the French knots in mauve silk buttonhole twist.
9. Using the thread colors indicated in the supplies list, sew on the purple frosted and pearlized glass beads, the large teal and pink glass beads, and the pearls.

The completed vest.

Thread and Floss

1 skein green embroidery floss (worked with three strands)

1 card mauve silk buttonhole twist

1 card yellow gold silk buttonhole twist

1 card green silk buttonhole twist

Mauve thread (for the purple and pink glass beads)

Teal thread (for the teal glass beads)

Ecru thread (for the pearls)

Embellishments

Glass Beads

16 purple frosted

30 purple pearlized

12 large pink

5 large teal

20 gold metallic

Pearls

6 8mm

8 4mm

2 12mm

Miscellaneous

White fabric pencil

Fabric eraser

DESIGN 2: LOWER LEFT LAPEL

1. Stitch one Japanese ribbon stitch flower each in 7mm purple, light purple, and lilac silk ribbons.
2. Stitch one three-petal Japanese ribbon stitch bud each with 7mm coral and light purple silk ribbons.
3. Stitch the lazy daisy leaves with 4mm grass green silk ribbon.
4. Stitch the twisted Japanese ribbon stitch leaves and leaf stitches with 4mm light green silk ribbon.
5. Stitch the stem stitch stems with green embroidery floss.
6. Stitch the Japanese ribbon stitch leaves on either side of the lower right-hand stem with 4mm grass green silk ribbon.
7. Stitch the French knot clusters with 4mm purple, lavender, and yellow silk ribbons. Within each cluster, stitch French knots with mauve and gold silk buttonhole twist.
8. Stitch the two lines of feather stitches with green silk buttonhole twist.
9. Add French knots in 4mm white silk ribbon to the tips of the feather stitches.
10. Using the thread colors indicated in the supplies list and a #10 beading needle, sew on the purple frosted and pearlized glass beads, the gold metallic glass beads, the large teal and pink glass beads, and the pearls.

DESIGN 3: UPPER RIGHT LAPEL

1. Stitch one Japanese ribbon stitch flower each with 7mm dark teal, light teal, and light orange silk ribbons.
2. Stitch the stem stitches with green embroidery floss.
3. Stitch Japanese ribbon stitch leaves on either side of each descending stem with 4mm pink, lilac, and purple silk ribbons.
4. Stitch Japanese ribbon stitch leaves on either side of each ascending stem, using 4mm grass green silk ribbon for one, and 4mm light green silk ribbon for the other.
5. Stitch the feather stitches with green silk buttonhole twist.
6. Add French knots with 4mm white silk ribbon to the tips of the feather stitches.
7. Stitch the French knot clusters with mauve silk buttonhole twist.
8. Using the thread colors indicated in the supplies list and using a #10 beading needle, sew on the purple, gold metallic, and teal glass beads and the pearls.

DESIGN 4: LOWER RIGHT LAPEL

1. Stitch the twisted Japanese ribbon stitch leaves with 4mm light green silk ribbon.
2. Stitch the stem stitches with green embroidery floss.
3. Stitch the feather stitches with green silk buttonhole twist.
4. Add French knots in 4mm white silk ribbon to the tips of the feather stitches.
5. Stitch the French knot clusters with 4mm lavender and yellow silk ribbons and mauve silk buttonhole twist.
6. Using the thread colors indicated in the supplies list, sew on the glass beads.

POCKET FLAPS

1. Stitch the Japanese ribbon stitch flowers with 7mm purple, light purple, and light orange silk ribbons.
2. Stitch the feather stitches with green silk buttonhole twist.
3. Add French knots in 4mm white silk ribbon to the tips of the feather stitches.
4. Stitch the French knots with mauve silk buttonhole twist.
5. Sew on the glass beads.
6. Repeat steps 1 through 5 on the other pocket flap.

A detail of the pocket
flap (right) and Design 1
on the upper left lapel
(below right).

Home Decor

Silk ribbon embroidery can be worked in a number of styles, offering stitchers a range of attractive decorating possibilities for the home. Ribbon-embroidered items fit particularly well within the Victorian and English country garden decors that are currently popular. Just a touch of ribbon embroidery can lend a feeling of luxury and timelessness to a room. The projects in this chapter are easy to create and will give you and your family years of pleasure.

Brocade Sachet

SKILL LEVEL
Beginner

TIME TO COMPLETE
2 hours

STITCHES USED
Bradford rose
Leaf stitch
Stem stitch
Straight stitch
Japanese ribbon stitch
French knot

SUPPLIES
Project
Purchased sachet
OR
One 6- × 14-inch piece of
bronze brocade
One 3- × 12-inch piece of
lace
1 yard ¹/₂-inch double-
sided ivory satin ribbon
Stitch Pattern
Page 131
Silk Ribbon
2¹/₂ yards 4mm mauve
16 inches 4mm burgundy
16 inches 4mm green
16 inches 4mm light blue
16 inches 4mm dark blue
16 inches 4mm pale
yellow
Thread
1 card pale green silk
buttonhole twist
1 card mauve silk
buttonhole twist
Miscellaneous
Water-soluble marking pen
4-inch hoop

Sachets are at once practical and extravagant, providing a sensible way to use fabric remnants while serving as elegant gifts and decorative touches. For this project, I selected a soft bronze brocade to make a 5¹/₂- × 6¹/₂-inch bag. Fill your sachet with dried lavender, or use it to present a small yet precious gift.

TRANSFER METHOD

- *If you're stitching a purchased sachet,* use the water-soluble marking pen to mark the centers of the Bradford roses and the lines of the stem stitches on the front of the bag.
- *If you're making a sachet,* use the water-soluble marking pen to draw a 6¹/₂- × 14-inch rectangle on the right side of the fabric, then divide it to make two 6¹/₂- × 7-inch blocks. Mark the elements of the stitch pattern in the center of the top block.

After the stitching is complete, remove any visible markings with a damp cloth.

STITCHING INSTRUCTIONS

1. Using burgundy silk ribbon for the French knot centers and mauve silk ribbon for the surrounding whip stitches, stitch the four Bradford roses. Note that one rose has one tier of whip stitches, two have two tiers, and one has three tiers.
2. Stitch the leaf stitches with green silk ribbon.
3. Stitch the stem stitch stems with green silk buttonhole twist.
4. Stitch the stem stitch tendril that curls above the roses with mauve silk buttonhole twist. Add the small straight stitch stems that jut off the tendril with mauve silk buttonhole twist.
5. Stitch the Japanese ribbon stitch buds, using light blue silk ribbon for the center petal and dark blue silk ribbon for the surrounding petals.
6. Stitch the French knot buds with pale yellow silk ribbon.

FINISHING THE SACHET

If you're making your own sachet, follow the instructions below using a ¹/₂-inch seam allowance.

1. Cut the entire 6¹/₂- × 14-inch block from the fabric. Fold over a ¹/₂ inch of fabric at the top edge, then press and sew it. Align the lace with the edge of the seam, right sides together, then pin and sew it in place. Repeat on the other edge of the fabric.
2. Fold the fabric in half along the width, right sides together. Sew the side seams, then turn the bag inside out.
3. Fold the satin ribbon in half, mark its center point, then stitch it at its center point to the back of the sachet. Tie the ribbon in a bow.

*(Right) The completed
sachet, with a detail of
the stitching showing three
sizes of Bradford roses
(below right).*

Porcelain Jar with Moiré Cover

SKILL LEVEL
Beginner

TIME TO COMPLETE
2 hours

STITCHES USED
Spider web rose
Padded straight stitch
French knot
Lazy daisy
Stem stitch
Straight stitch

SUPPLIES

Project
Purchased medium-size
3-inch round ivory
porcelain jar kit
One 6-inch square of
peach moiré fabric
One 4-inch square of
polyester batting OR fleece

Stitch Pattern
Page 131

Silk Ribbon
1 1/2 yards 4mm dark
purple
16 inches 4mm terracotta
16 inches 4mm dark rose
16 inches 4mm pale
yellow
16 inches 4mm dark olive
green
10 inches 4mm lavender

Thread
1 card celery green silk
buttonhole twist
1 spool terracotta thread
1 spool ecru thread
1 spool purple thread

Embellishments
6 oval 1/4-inch pearls
9 small purple glass beads

Miscellaneous
Tracing paper
Permanent black fineline
marker
Tulle netting
Water-soluble marking pen
4-inch hoop

This easy-to-make project creates an heirloom-quality gift suitable for any occasion. The porcelain jar shown opposite is available in a kit that includes assembly instructions for the cover. Once the fabric has been stitched, the cover can be assembled in just a few minutes.

The term "moiré" (French for "watered silk") refers to the ridges within the fabric that create waves of reflected light. Choose the fabric and ribbon colors to suit a room's decor or an individual's taste. To create a wedding keepsake, stitch the design on white or ivory fabric with the bridal party's colors.

TRANSFER METHOD
Using the tulle netting transfer method (see page 24), lightly trace the design on the fabric with the water-soluble marking pen. After the stitching is complete, remove any visible marks with a damp cotton swab. (Note that moiré has a tendency to mark with water. If this should happen, simply spritz the entire piece of fabric evenly with water and the marks will disappear.)

STITCHING INSTRUCTIONS
1. Stitch the spider web rose with terracotta silk ribbon, using the terracotta thread to create the foundation spokes.
2. Stitch the padded straight stitch buds with terracotta silk ribbon.
3. Stitch the five-petal French knot flower and one of the five-petal lazy daisy flowers with dark rose silk ribbon. Add a French knot to the center of each flower with pale yellow silk ribbon.
4. Stitch one each of the two remaining lazy daisy flowers with dark purple and lavender silk ribbons, using pale yellow silk ribbon to stitch their French knot centers.
5. Stitch the French knot grape clusters with dark purple silk ribbon.
6. Stitch the sprinkle of French knots on the right side of the composition with pale yellow silk ribbon.
7. Stitch the large lazy daisy leaves with dark olive green silk ribbon.
8. Stitch the stem stitches and the small lazy daisy leaves with celery green silk buttonhole twist. Add a tiny straight stitch calyx and stamen to each terracotta silk ribbon bud.
9. Using a #10 beading needle and the ecru or purple threads, stitch the pearls and glass beads into place.

ASSEMBLY
Follow the manufacturer's instructions to assemble the jar lid. Note that fleece will give the lid more dimension than polyester batting.

*(Above) The assembled
jar, with a detail of the
stitched cover (right).*

Eyelet Lampshade

SKILL LEVEL
Beginner

TIME TO COMPLETE
3 hours

STITCHES USED
Spider web rose

Lazy daisy

French knot

Stem stitch

Pistil stitch

Padded straight stitch

Japanese ribbon stitch

Plume stitch

SUPPLIES

Project
One adhesive-backed
5- × 5-inch lampshade

One 6- × 14-inch piece of
white cotton eyelet

Stitch Pattern
Page 131

Silk Ribbon
1 yard 4mm mauve

1 yard 4mm light mauve

1 yard 4mm pale yellow

1 yard 4mm light teal

16 inches 4mm teal

Thread and Floss
1 skein teal embroidery
floss (worked with two
strands)

1 spool mauve thread

Embellishments
17 inches of 1/2-inch mint
green braid

12 inches of 1-inch mint
green braid with lace edge

Miscellaneous
Tracing paper

Permanent black fineline
marker

Tulle netting

Water-soluble marking pen

Low-temperature glue gun
and glue sticks

The small eyelet lampshade in this project makes a charming statement anywhere it is placed. Use it to accent a dressing table lamp or to shade a hallway night-light.

If possible, use lace with 2 inches of space between the patterns to give the stitching an adequate foundation. Because the weight of the lace is relatively light and the stitching will be illuminated from the back, you must minimize ribbon bulk on the reverse of the fabric. Instead of softly knotting the ribbon when threading the needle, leave a 1-inch tail on the back of the fabric, then anchor it in place with the next stitch. When the stitching is complete, clip all the loose ribbon ends and neaten the back of the piece before gluing it to the shade.

The stitch design would also work well along the top border of a fabric picture frame or the front of a sweater or camisole. To create a stunning hatband, stitch the design on a 3-inch-wide grosgrain or French ribbon. Select a ribbon palette of pale pastels to enhance the bodice of a dress for a holiday or special occasion.

TRANSFER METHOD
Using the tulle netting transfer method (see page 24), lightly trace the design on the center of the eyelet lace with the water-soluble marking pen. After the stitching is complete, remove any visible marks with a damp cotton swab.

STITCHING INSTRUCTIONS
1. Stitch the spider web roses with mauve silk ribbon, using the mauve thread to create the foundation spokes.
2. Stitch the lazy daisy flowers with light mauve silk ribbon. Add French knot centers with pale yellow silk ribbon.
3. Stitch the lazy daisy leaves with light teal silk ribbon.
4. Stitch the stem stitch stems and vines and the pistil stitches with teal floss.
5. Stitch the padded straight stitch buds and the French knot grape clusters with light teal silk ribbon.
6. Stitch the Japanese ribbon stitch leaves and the French knots at each end of the two outermost vines with teal silk ribbon.
7. Stitch the five-petal French knot flowers and the two single French knots between the spider web roses with light mauve silk ribbon. Use mauve silk ribbon to stitch the center of each flower.
8. Stitch the plume stitches with pale yellow silk ribbon.

ASSEMBLY
1. Following the manufacturer's instructions, apply the stitched eyelet to the shade, positioning the design so that the raw edges of the fabric can be folded together at the back and turned under. Use the glue gun to glue the folded eyelet to the back of the shade. Let dry.
2. Glue the lace-edged braid around the top of the shade, and the mint green braid around the bottom. Align the ends of the braid with the folded eyelet at the back of the shade.

*(Right) The completed
lampshade, with a
detail of the stitch design
(below right).*

Tasseled Moiré and Lace Pillow

SKILL LEVEL
Intermediate

TIME TO COMPLETE
3 hours

STITCHES USED
Folded rose
Japanese ribbon stitch

SUPPLIES

Project
Purchased rectangular pillow with tassels (with a zipper closure so that the pillow form can be removed)

Stitch Patterns
Pages 132 and 133

Silk Ribbon
1 yard 7mm light forest green

Satin Ribbon
2 yards 1-inch double-sided ivory

2 yards 1/4-inch double-sided ivory

1 yard 1-inch double-sided bronze

20 inches 5/8-inch double-sided ivory

Embroidery Floss
1 skein ecru (worked with two strands)

Embellishments
43 4mm pearls

Miscellaneous
Water-soluble marking pen
4-inch hoop

This project is an exercise in folding the perfect rose. Working with wide satin ribbon makes the process of rolling, folding, and stitching easier. The pillow I purchased for this project was large enough (12 × 16 inches) to accommodate the exaggerated size of the roses and the clustered configuration I had in mind, and the pattern of the lace provided adequate visual contrast for the soft floral forms. If you can't find a ready-made pillow that's decorated similarly, purchase one of the same size and dimensions, along with a piece of scalloped lace measuring 3 1/2 × 19 inches. (In any event, make sure the pillow form is removable.) Tack the lace to the pillow with ecru floss, and begin stitching.

Due to the dimensions of the roses, this pillow is not recommended for dry cleaning.

TRANSFER METHOD
Use the water-soluble marking pen to mark the points at which the folded roses will be tacked to the lace. If needed, add sketch lines to mark the path of the narrow satin ribbon. Note, however, that this ribbon should be applied in a freeform manner, as long as it is evenly distributed among the clusters of folded roses.

STITCHING INSTRUCTIONS
1. Using the 1-inch ivory satin ribbon, fold and stitch five roses. Set them aside.
2. Using the 1-inch bronze satin ribbon, fold and stitch four roses. Set them aside.
3. Fold and stitch two roses using the 5/8-inch ivory ribbon. Set them aside.
4. Mount the fabric on the hoop. Tack one large ivory rose and two large bronze roses to the center of the lace strip, then tack the two smaller ivory roses to the lace on either side of the cluster.
5. Tack a trio of roses—two ivory and one bronze—on either side of the central cluster.
6. Stitch the Japanese ribbon stitch leaves with 7mm green silk ribbon.
7. Remove the hoop. Use a #10 beading needle and the ecru floss to tack the 1/4-inch ivory satin ribbon and the pearls into place. Use 8-inch pieces of ribbon between and on either side of each cluster, and 4-inch pieces for the shorter lengths that branch above or below. Begin by tacking each piece of ribbon beneath its corresponding cluster. As you twist and curl each piece according to the pattern, tack it in place with a pearl.
8. Remove the hoop marks with a light pressing, then re-insert the form back into the pillow.

(Above) The completed
pillow, with a detail of
the right-hand cluster
of roses (right).

Broadcloth Tea Cozy

SKILL LEVEL

Intermediate

TIME TO COMPLETE

8 hours

STITCHES USED

French knot

Pistil stitch

Japanese ribbon stitch

Satin stitch

Lazy daisy

Leaf stitch

Decorative lazy daisy

Stem stitch

Feather stitch

Whip stitch

Padded straight stitch

Straight stitch

SUPPLIES

Project

Purchased tea cozy OR
English Cottage Tea Cozy
pattern from Folkwear
Patterns

1/3 yard fleece batting

1/3 yard ivory broadcloth

1 spool ivory thread

Stitch Pattern

Page 134

Silk Ribbon

3 yards 4mm dark red

2 yards 4mm royal blue

2 yards 4mm coral

1 1/2 yards 4mm purple

1 1/3 yards 4mm deep coral

1 yard 4mm gold

1 yard 4mm peach

24 inches 4mm olive

16 inches 4mm
cornflower blue

16 inches 4mm dark olive

10 inches 4mm ivory

Thread and Floss

1 skein blue embroidery
floss

Silk Buttonhole Twist

1 card yellow gold silk

1 card green

Miscellaneous

Tracing paper

Black fineline marker

Tulle netting

Water-soluble marking pen

The term "broadcloth" refers to fabrics with a twilled weave. The cotton broadcloth I used for this project is heavier than linen, has more body, and doesn't wrinkle as easily. Regardless of whether you're making your own tea cozy or stitching on a ready-made one, you must wash and dry the fabric to allow for shrinkage and to remove sizing, and check the dark red, royal blue, and gold ribbons for colorfastness before you begin stitching. (See "Testing Ribbons for Colorfastness," page 27.) If the bleeding or running persists, take the safe route and use lighter shades in the same color family, but not before testing them as well.

TRANSFER METHOD

Using the tulle netting transfer method (see page 24), lightly trace the design with the water-soluble marking pen on the center of the tea cozy or on the right side of one of the pieces of fabric cut to the pattern. After the stitching is complete, remove any visible marks with a damp cotton swab.

STITCHING INSTRUCTIONS

1. Stitch the French knot centers of the pistil stitch flowers that compose the basket with royal blue silk ribbon. Stitch the surrounding pistil stitches with two strands of blue embroidery floss.
2. Stitch the petals of the large Japanese ribbon stitch daisy with gold silk ribbon. Fill its center with satin stitches in ivory silk ribbon, then encircle them with French knots in peach silk ribbon.
3. Stitch the five-petal lazy daisy flowers with dark red silk ribbon. Add French knot centers with deep coral silk ribbon.
4. Stitch the Japanese ribbon stitch bachelor's button on the right and the three buds on the left with cornflower blue silk ribbon. Fill in the center of the bachelor's button with a large cluster of double-wrap French knots in yellow gold silk buttonhole twist.
5. Stitch the leaf stitch that extends above the bachelor's button with dark olive silk ribbon.
6. Stitch the French knot grape clusters with purple silk ribbon and the French knots scattered throughout the design with purple, cornflower blue, and coral silk ribbons.
7. Stitch the decorative lazy daisies with deep coral (for the loops) and dark red (for the straight stitches) silk ribbons.
8. Stitch the stem stitches and feather stitches with green silk buttonhole twist.
9. Stitch the Japanese ribbon stitch leaves with olive and dark olive silk ribbons.
10. Stitch the whip stitches with gold silk ribbon.
11. Stitch the padded straight stitch bluebells with royal blue silk ribbon, then add a small horizontal straight stitch in dark red silk ribbon at the bottom of each one. Add pistil stitch stamens with yellow gold silk buttonhole twist.
12. Stitch the two Japanese ribbon stitch buds on the right with peach silk ribbon.
13. Stitch the stem stitch basket handle with six strands of blue floss.

ASSEMBLY

If you're making your tea cozy from a pattern, assemble the fabric and batting according to the pattern instructions. Press the completed tea cozy.

(Above) The completed tea cozy, with a detail of a Japanese ribbon stitch bachelor's button, padded straight stitch bluebells, a spray of red lazy daisies, and a Japanese ribbon stitch daisy (right).

Damask Hand Mirror

SKILL LEVEL
Intermediate

TIME TO COMPLETE
16 hours

STITCHES USED
Satin stitch
Japanese ribbon stitch
Lazy daisy
Stem stitch
Pistil stitch
Straight stitch
French knot

SUPPLIES

Project
Purchased hand mirror kit
(to make a 6- × 12-inch
mirror)
1/4 yard ivory damask
One 6- × 12-inch piece of
batting

Stitch Pattern
Page 135

Silk Ribbon
7mm Width
1 1/2 yards orange
2/3 yard olive green
4mm Width
1 1/2 yards brown
1 1/2 yards gold
1 yard olive green
1 yard light green
1 yard rust
1 yard dark orange
1 yard pale orange

Embroidery Floss
1 skein silver marlitt
1 skein bronze marlitt

Embellishments
10-inch strand of 4mm
ivory pearls
30 inches of 3/8-inch ivory
braid
One 4-inch ivory tassel

Miscellaneous
Tracing paper
Permanent black fineline
marker
Tulle netting
Water-soluble marking pen
Low-temperature glue gun
and glue sticks

I adapted the stitch design for this hand mirror from a detail of a mid-18th century embroidered French lingerie bag. I chose a ribbon palette of autumn colors, but any color scheme would stitch a beautiful project. For the fabric, I used the damask from the waistcoat project (see page 76).

The mirror is assembled with a kit that can be purchased in fine sewing stores. If you don't have a kit, you'll need two pieces of heavy cardboard and a small piece of mirrored glass.

TRANSFER METHOD

Using the tulle netting transfer method (see page 24), lightly trace the design on the center of the damask with the water-soluble marking pen. After the stitching is complete, remove any visible marks with a damp cotton swab.

STITCHING INSTRUCTIONS

1. Use the silver marlitt to stitch the satin stitch ribbon. Before threading the needle, separate all four strands of the floss, then put them back together. This increases the marlitt's width, resulting in fuller stitches and more uniform coverage of the fabric.
2. Stitch the Japanese ribbon stitch chrysanthemum petals with 7mm orange silk ribbon.
3. Stitch the Japanese ribbon stitch leaves with 7mm olive green silk ribbon.
4. Stitch the lazy daisy leaves with 4mm olive green and light green silk ribbons.
5. Stitch the lazy daisy cattail spikes with 4mm brown and gold silk ribbons.
6. Stitch the stem stitch stems with two strands of bronze marlitt.
7. Stitch the lazy daisy wheat kernels with brown, gold, and rust silk ribbons.
8. Stitch the pistil stitch and straight stitch accents with bronze marlitt.
9. Stitch the French knot centers of the Japanese ribbon stitch chrysanthemums with 4mm dark orange and pale orange silk ribbons.

ASSEMBLY

1. Assemble the mirror according to the kit instructions. (Note that batting is used to create dimension only on the back of the handle, *not* under the mirror.)
2. Use the glue gun to affix the string of pearls around the perimeter of the mirror.
3. Glue the braided trim around the edge of the frame, then glue the tassel to the bottom of the handle.

(Above) The completed hand mirror, with a detail of the three Japanese ribbon stitch chrysanthemums (right).

Braid-Edged Moiré Pillow

SKILL LEVEL
Intermediate

TIME TO COMPLETE
18 hours

STITCHES USED
Loop flower
French knot
Padded straight stitch
Japanese ribbon stitch
Lazy daisy
Pistil stitch

SUPPLIES

Project
Purchased 14-inch square pillow (with a zipper closure so that the pillow form can be removed)

Stitch Pattern
Page 136

Silk Ribbon
3 yards 7mm light coral
3 yards 4mm pale yellow
3 yards 4mm ivory
2 yards 4mm mauve
1½ yards 4mm light coral
1 yard 4mm peach

Embroidery Floss
1 skein celery green (worked with two strands)
1 skein hunter green (worked with two strands)
1 skein ecru (worked with three strands)

Miscellaneous
Tracing paper
Permanent black fineline marker
Tulle netting
Water-soluble marking pen
5-inch wooden hoop OR an 8-inch Q-snap

Although a stylish moiré with a fleur-de-lis pattern was used for this project, the classic oval embroidery design would work well on any fabric and for many occasions; on a christening pillow, for example, or as a frame for a monogram or floral design.

When you're done stitching for the day, remove the hoop to prevent excessive creasing.

TRANSFER METHOD
Using the tulle netting transfer method (see page 24), lightly trace the design on the center of the fabric with the water-soluble marking pen. After the stitching is complete, remove any visible marks with a damp cotton swab. (Note that moiré has a tendency to mark with water. If this should happen, simply spritz the entire pillow evenly with water and the marks will disappear.)

STITCHING INSTRUCTIONS
1. Stitch the loop flowers with 7mm light coral silk ribbon.
2. Use ecru floss to stitch three French knots in the center of each loop flower.
3. Stitch the French knots with 4mm pale yellow and mauve silk ribbons.
4. Stitch the padded straight stitch buds with 4mm light coral silk ribbon.
5. Stitch the Japanese ribbon stitch flowers with 4mm pale yellow silk ribbon.
6. Add a French knot to the center of each Japanese ribbon stitch flower with 4mm light coral silk ribbon.
7. Use both shades of green floss to stitch the lazy daisy leaves.
8. Stitch the pistil stitch accents with ecru floss.

CARE AND CLEANING
To remove hoop marks, place the pillowcase face down on a fluffy towel. Hold a hot iron slightly above the design and allow the steam to remove the creases. (A product called Velvaboard, which is designed for pressing napped fabrics, is an excellent alternative to the towel. See page 28.)

Dry cleaning is not recommended, as some fabrics shrink when dry-cleaned and the pressing system will flatten the loop flowers. If the flowers flatten when pressed with an iron, simply touch them with a damp cotton swab and they will spring back.

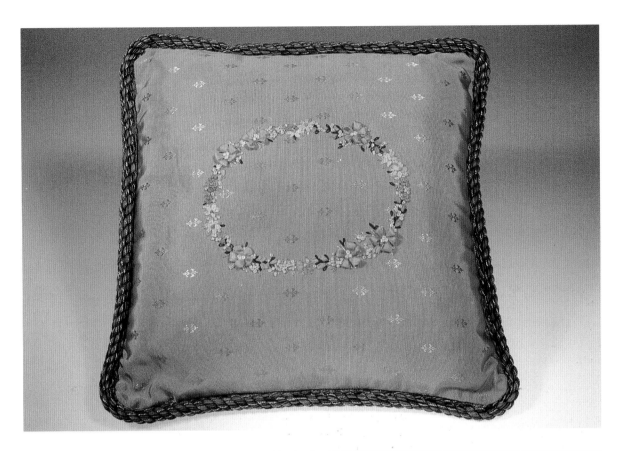

(Above) The completed pillow, with a detail showing two loop flowers with French knot centers surrounded by clusters of French knots and lazy daisy leaves (right).

Framed Dresden Vase

This framed piece would complement any formal room setting. To enhance the dimensional look of the ribbon embroidery, a polymer clay vase was designed to hold the roses, and a tiny "tablecloth" of 100-year-old lace completes the still life. If you prefer not to work with polymer clay, you can handpaint or appliqué a fabric vase (see instructions on page 100). Compared with the wider satin ribbons (see page 90), the slickness and small scale of 7mm silk ribbon make the folding process more difficult and time-consuming.

TRANSFER METHOD

Use the water-soluble marking pen to mark the points at which the folded roses will be tacked to the silk, the lines of the stem stitches, and the outlines of the vase and the lace.

STITCHING INSTRUCTIONS

1. Working with 7mm widths only, fold seven pink, four lavender, and three ivory roses. Use a #7 beading needle and thread in a color similar to that of each ribbon to secure the petals and to stitch the completed roses in place on the background.
2. Stitch the French knot loop stitches with 4mm lavender silk ribbon. Make each loop approximately 1/4 inch long, and position the French knot at the end, rather than in the center, of the loop.
3. Stitch the lazy daisy leaves immediately surrounding the bouquet with 4mm green silk ribbon.
4. Stitch the padded straight stitch buds with 4mm lavender and ivory silk ribbons.
5. Stitch the Japanese ribbon stitch calla lilies with 7mm lavender silk ribbon.
6. Use celery green silk buttonhole twist to stitch the straight stitch stems, calyxes, and stamens that accent the padded straight stitch buds and the Japanese ribbon stitch calla lilies.
7. Stitch the lazy daisy leaves and the pistil stitches with celery green silk buttonhole twist.
8. Stitch the single-wrap French knots with pale yellow and mauve silk buttonhole twist.
9. Turn the edges of the lace under to hide the raw edges, lightly dot each of the four corners with glue, then position the lace on the background.

MAKING THE VASE

There are three ways to make the vase that holds the rose bouquet: by molding and stamping polymer clay, or by painting or appliquéing a fabric vase. If your vase shape is fabric, it should be glued or appliquéd to the background before the piece is framed. In contrast, the weight of the polymer clay vase prevents it from being applied to the background fabric until after the piece has been framed. See page 100 for detailed instructions on making the vase and finishing the picture.

A detail of the rose bouquet featuring a polymer clay vase. Vase designed by Barbara Quast.

VASE SUPPLIES

Polymer Clay

White polymer clay (such as Fimo, Friendly Clay, Sculpey)

Rolling pin or dowel

Vase rubber stamp (SK125) from the Floral Bouquet Rubber Stamp Set by Personal Stamp Exchange

Royal blue water-based brush marker

Craft knife

Oven or toaster oven

FolkArt Spray Clearcote Hi-Shine Brilliant Glaze (784), Deep Gloss Finish by Plaid Enterprises

Fabric Painting

Scrap of tight-weave white or ivory medium-weight fabric (such as cotton twill or damask)

000 liner brush

Royal blue acrylic paint

Fray Check

White dimensional fabric paint (optional)

Appliqué

3- × 4-inch piece of blue-and-white floral or toile de jouy fabric

Betweens #10 (hand-appliqué or quilting needle)

Size 50 or 100 silk thread (in a color that matches the appliqué fabric)

Needle threader

POLYMER CLAY

Polymer clay is a versatile plastic-based material that is soft and moldable at room temperature and hardens into a permanent plastic when baked.

1. Knead the clay until it is soft and pliable. Roll out the clay to $1/16$ inch.

2. Use the royal blue marker to ink the rubber stamp die. Apply the ink only to the decorative design within the vase, avoiding its outline. To remoisten the ink, breathe on the die as if you were fogging a mirror, then stamp the image on the clay.

3. Leaving a wide border around its edge, cut around the vase with a craft knife. To avoid smearing the ink and distorting the vase's shape, cut the clay away in wedges instead of outlining the vase with the knife blade.

4. Without touching the ink, place the vase on a ceramic or glass baking dish. Bake the vase according to the package instructions; let cool.

5. Seal the color on the vase with a light coat of glaze. Let dry. Repeat to add four more light coats.

FABRIC PAINTING

1. Trace the vase pattern onto the fabric with a water-soluble marking pen.

2. Use the liner brush and acrylic paint thinned with water to paint a floral design within the vase's outline. (If you prefer, you can stamp the image with fabric stamping ink.) Let dry.

3. Cut the vase shape out of the fabric. (If you're planning to appliqué the vase, leave a $1/4$- to an $1/8$-inch border around the shape. See "Appliqué," below.) Treat the cut edge of the vase with Fray Check to keep the fabric from raveling.

4. Apply the painted fabric vase to the background with E6000 or with an outline of dimensional fabric paint.

APPLIQUÉ

The term appliqué (from the French word *appliquer,* "to put on") refers to the process of applying a cutout of one fabric (in this case, the vase) to the background of another (the fabric that also supports the ribbon embroidery).

1. Trace the vase pattern onto the right side of the appliqué fabric. (The grain of the appliqué should align with the grain of the background fabric.) The outline of the vase will serve as the turning under or sewing line. To accommodate a seam allowance, cut $1/8$ to $1/4$ inch around the pattern line.

2. Pin the vase cutout to the background fabric over the vase outline. Baste the cutout in place with large, loose stitches.

3. Thread the needle with about 18 inches of silk thread. Fold the seam allowance under so that the pattern line is just slightly underneath the fabric. Come up through the background fabric at the edge of the fold, then go back down directly beside that point.

4. Take about an $1/8$-inch stitch on the reverse of the fabric, then repeat step 3. As you continue to blindstitch the perimeter of the vase shape, hold down about 1 inch of the seam allowance at a time with your thumb.

FINISHING THE PICTURE

1. Have the finished piece professionally mounted and framed using acid-free materials.

2. Dot the back of the baked polymer clay vase with several droplets of E6000 adhesive. Position the vase within the pattern lines and immediately beneath the bouquet so that the loop flowers hang over its edge.

3. Allow the glue to set for 24 hours before hanging.

The completed framed piece. If desired, sign the back of the framed piece, noting the date and where it was stitched. If you intend to give it as a gift, indicate the name of the recipient.

Special Occasions

The projects in this chapter were designed to commemorate some of life's special moments. By creating family heirlooms, we revive our cherished memories and convey the significance of the past to those who follow us. When heirlooms are shared over generations, they take on lives of their own, offering past, present, and future in their gathered reminiscences and in the celebrations of tomorrow they evoke.

Christmas Ornaments

SKILL LEVEL
Beginner

TIME TO COMPLETE
1 hour (each ornament)

STITCHES USED
All Three Ornaments
Lazy daisy
French knot

Heart Ornament Only
Leaf stitch
Stem stitch
Pistil stitch

Boot and Bell
Ornaments Only
Japanese ribbon stitch

STITCH PATTERNS
Page 138

TRANSFER TOOLS
Heart and Bell
Ornaments
Tracing paper
Permanent black fineline
marker
Tulle netting
Water-soluble marking pen

Boot Ornament
White fabric pencil
Fabric eraser

**MISCELLANEOUS
SUPPLIES**
For All Three Ornaments
4-inch hoop
Three 6-inch squares of
batting (one for each
ornament)
Low-temperature glue gun
and glue sticks

These charming ornaments, which can also double as trimming for wrapped gifts, are extremely easy to make and can be enjoyed year after year. In fact, they're so easy to stitch that I use them to teach my 8- and 9-year-old students basic ribbon embroidery. Even if you're just starting out, share what you know about silk ribbon with a young friend or relative. It's a great way to review and reinforce what you've learned.

You can find the Pres-On Products used to make these ornaments in fabric, craft, and hobby stores.

TRANSFER METHODS

Place the Pres-On ornament shape in the center of its square of fabric. Lightly trace the design with a water-soluble marking pen or white fabric pencil (see instructions below), then transfer the stitch pattern as follows:

- *For the heart and bell ornaments.* Using the tulle netting transfer method (see page 24), lightly trace the design on the fabric with the water-soluble marking pen. After the stitching is complete, remove any visible marks with a damp cotton swab.
- *For the boot ornament.* Use the white fabric pencil to lightly mark the centers of the Japanese ribbon stitch flowers. After the stitching is complete, remove any visible marks with the fabric eraser.

ASSEMBLING THE ORNAMENTS

When you're done stitching, follow the manufacturer's instructions to cut the square of batting to the shape of the ornament. Glue the batting to the cardboard, then lay the embroidered piece over the batting. Fold the overhanging fabric to the back of the cardboard and glue it in place. Repeat for the second cardboard shape using a matching piece of fabric but no batting. Finish each ornament as directed below.

The completed ornaments.

Project

Pres-On Products heart shape

One 12-inch square of red moiré

Silk Ribbon

1 1/2 yards 4mm forest green

1 yard 4mm white

1 yard 4mm yellow

Embroidery Floss

1 skein green (worked with two strands)

Embellishments

7 inches 1/4-inch red grosgrain ribbon

15 inches 1/4-inch red-and-green braid

2 1/2-inch red tassel

HEART ORNAMENT

STITCHING INSTRUCTIONS

1. Stitch the lazy daisy flowers with 4mm white silk ribbon.
2. Stitch the French knots with 4mm yellow silk ribbon.
3. Stitch the leaf stitches with 4mm forest green silk ribbon.
4. Stitch the stem stitches and pistil stitches with green embroidery floss.

FINISHING THE ORNAMENT

1. Glue the two shapes wrong sides together.
2. Glue on the grosgrain ribbon loop and the tassel.
3. Glue the red-and-green braid around the perimeter of the ornament.

The heart ornament.

BOOT ORNAMENT

Project

Pres-On Products boot
shape

12-inch square of green
velvet

Silk Ribbon

1 yard 4mm mauve

1 yard 4mm light green

1/2 yard 4mm ivory

Thread

1 yard heavy gold metallic
braid

Embellishments

4 inches 1-inch gathered
ivory lace

1 1/2-inch ivory tassel

26 inches 1/8-inch metallic
gold-and-ivory braid

STITCHING INSTRUCTIONS

1. Stitch the Japanese ribbon stitch flower at the curve of the heel with ivory silk ribbon.
2. Stitch the two remaining Japanese ribbon stitch flowers with mauve silk ribbon.
3. Stitch the lazy daisy leaves with light green silk ribbon.
4. Stitch the French knots with gold metallic braid.

FINISHING THE ORNAMENT

1. Glue the two shapes wrong sides together.
2. Glue the gathered strip of lace to the top of the boot front. Glue a 4-inch strip of gold-and-ivory braid along the top edge of the lace strip.
3. To create the loop, fold a 4-inch piece of gold-and-ivory braid in half, then glue the ends to the top left edge of the boot. Glue the ivory tassel immediately under the loop.
4. Finish the edge of the ornament with the gold-and-ivory braid.

The boot ornament.

BELL ORNAMENT
SUPPLIES

Project

Pres-On Products bell shape

12-inch square of white damask

Silk Ribbon

1½ yards 4mm red

1 yard 4mm bright yellow

26 inches 4mm dark green

16 inches 4mm light green

Embellishments

16 inches ¼-inch lace

15-inch strand of 4mm white fused pearls

6 inches ¼-inch red grosgrain ribbon

BELL ORNAMENT

STITCHING INSTRUCTIONS

1. Stitch the lazy daisy flowers and the lazy daisy and Japanese ribbon stitch bow with red silk ribbon.
2. Stitch the Japanese ribbon stitch leaves that form the wreath shape with dark green silk ribbon.
3. Stitch the Japanese ribbon stitch leaves that accent the lazy daisy flowers with light green silk ribbon.
4. Stitch the French knots with bright yellow silk ribbon.

FINISHING THE ORNAMENT

1. Glue the lace around the perimeter of the back of the embroidered shape. Gather the lace slightly to ease it around curves and corners.
2. Fold the piece of grosgrain ribbon in half, then glue the ends to the inside of the back of the ornament.
3. Glue the two shapes wrong sides together.
4. Glue the strand of pearls around the perimeter of the front of the ornament.

The bell ornament.

Bridal Sachet

SKILL LEVEL
Beginner

TIME TO COMPLETE
2 hours

STITCHES USED
Loop flower
French knot loop stitch
Lazy daisy
Stem stitch
Padded straight stitch
Straight stitch
French knot

SUPPLIES
Project
One 6- × 14-inch piece of
light blue silk
One 4- × 8-inch piece of
vintage ivory lace
1 yard 1-inch ivory double-
sided satin ribbon

Stitch Pattern
Page 139

Silk Ribbon
16 inches 4mm ivory
16 inches 4mm pale yellow
16 inches 4mm pale green
16 inches 4mm mauve

Thread and Floss
1 skein pale green floss
(worked with two strands)
1 skein mauve floss
(worked with two strands)
1 spool white thread

Embellishments
9 4mm pearls

Miscellaneous
Water-soluble marking pen
4-inch hoop

This lovely sachet can serve as the "something blue" that's a must for every bride. The fabric I selected for this project is a light blue silk delicately etched with a feather design. The size of the finished sachet is 4 × 6½ inches.

Fill your sachet with a delicate potpourri, or use it to present a special gift, such as a strand of heirloom pearls or a lacy antique white linen handkerchief.

TRANSFER METHOD
Fold the fabric in half along the width, wrong sides together. Use the water-soluble marking pen to lightly mark the centers of the two loop flowers and the lines of the stem stitches on one side of the fabric, either at the center or near the fold. After the stitching is complete, remove any visible markings with a damp cloth.

STITCHING INSTRUCTIONS
1. Stitch one each of the two loop flowers with the ivory and pale yellow silk ribbons.
2. Stitch the French knot loop stitches with ivory silk ribbon.
3. Stitch the lazy daisy leaves with pale green silk ribbon.
4. Stitch the stem stitches with pale green embroidery floss.
5. Stitch the padded straight stitch buds with pale yellow silk ribbon.
6. Add tiny straight stitch calyxes and stamens in green floss to each of the padded straight stitch buds.
7. Tie a three-loop bow with mauve silk ribbon, then tack it down to the right of the loop flowers. Tack down each tail of the bow with a French knot stitched with mauve embroidery floss.
8. Stitch the scattering of French knots with mauve embroidery floss.
9. Use a #10 beading needle and the white thread to stitch the pearls into position.

FINISHING THE SACHET
Use a ½-inch seam allowance when sewing the sachet.
1. Cut a ½ inch from either side of the fabric so that the width of the piece is 5 inches. Fold over a ½ inch of fabric at the top edge, then press and sew it. Align the lace with the edge of the seam, right sides together, then pin and sew it in place. Repeat on the other edge of the fabric.
2. Refold the fabric in half along the width, right sides together. Sew the side seams, then turn the bag inside out.
3. Fold the satin ribbon in half, mark its center point, then stitch it at its center point to the back of the sachet. Tie the ribbon in a bow.

(Right) The completed
sachet, with a detail
of the three-loop bow
(below right).

Ringbearer's Pillow

SKILL LEVEL
Beginner

TIME TO COMPLETE
4 hours

STITCHES USED
Straight stitch rose
Japanese ribbon stitch
Lazy daisy
Straight stitch
Feather stitch
French knot

SUPPLIES
Project
Purchased 10-inch-square wedding pillow (with a zipper closure so that the pillow form can be removed)
OR
Two 12-inch squares of ivory damask
1 1/2 yards of 3-inch-wide double ruffle ecru lace
1 1/2-yard strand of 4mm white fused pearls
Polyester fiberfill

Stitch Pattern
Page 139

Silk Ribbon
2 yards 4mm pink
1 yard 4mm hot pink
16 inches 4mm green
16 inches 4mm yellow
16 inches 4mm lavender
16 inches 4mm blue

Thread and Floss
1 skein green embroidery floss (worked with two strands)
1 spool ecru thread .

Embellishments
18 4mm pearls
8 yards 1/4-inch double-sided ivory satin ribbon

Miscellaneous
Tracing paper
Permanent black fineline marker
Tulle netting
Water-soluble marking pen
Beading wire

This ringbearer's pillow features a soft, heart-shaped wreath of flowers. This design can also be used to create a matching moneypurse; simply use the instructions for the bridal moneypurse (see pages 112–113) as a guide to purchasing fabric and assembling the purse.

TRANSFER METHOD
Using the tulle netting transfer method (see page 24), lightly trace the design on the pillow cover (or, if you're making your pillow from scratch, on the right side of one square of the damask) with the water-soluble marking pen. After the stitching is complete, remove any visible marks with a damp cotton swab.

STITCHING INSTRUCTIONS
1. Stitch the three straight stitch roses, starting with the large rose at the center. Use hot pink for the inner tiers of stitches and pink for the outer tiers. Leave enough space in the center of each rose to accommodate a single pearl.
2. Stitch the Japanese ribbon stitch leaves with green silk ribbon.
3. Stitch the lazy daisy buds with pink silk ribbon.
4. Stitch the straight stitches and feather stitches with green embroidery floss.
5. Stitch the French knots with yellow, lavender, and blue silk ribbons.
6. Stitch the pearls into place with the ecru thread and a #10 beading needle.

ASSEMBLING THE PILLOW
If you're making a pillow from scratch, follow all of the instructions below. If you're stitching a ready-made pillow cover, skip ahead to step 3.
1. Place the two damask squares right sides together. Stitch the edges of the pillow together, leaving a 5-inch opening on one side. Turn the pillow cover right side out, then stuff it with fiberfill. Whip stitch the opening closed.
2. Pin the lace to the edge of the pillow. Begin and end on the same corner, then trim the ends at a 45-degree angle. Using the ecru thread and small whip stitches, sew the lace to the pillow and finish the ends.
3. Align the end of the strand of fused pearls in a corner. Lay the strand over the stitched edge of the lace, then sew them into place with the ecru thread, taking a stitch every 1/2 inch. Stitch the strand all the way around the pillow, then trim it to finish at the corner.
4. Using the 1/4-inch ivory satin ribbon, make two bows with 12-inch tails for each corner of the pillow. Tie a soft knot in each tail. Wrap each pair of bows together with beading wire, twist the wire twice at the back, then cut it. Tack one double bow to each corner with ecru thread, making several tiny stitches.
5. If you want to secure the rings to surface of the pillow, complete this step: Take an additional 8 inches of 1/4-inch satin ribbon, then tack it at its center point to center of the double bow on the corner of the pillow closest to the design. Thread the ribbon through the rings, then tie a simple bow. Pull the ribbon's tail to release the rings.

(Above) The completed
pillow, with a detail of
the heart motif (right).

Bridal Moneypurse

SKILL LEVEL
Beginner

TIME TO COMPLETE
6 hours

STITCHES USED
Stem stitch
Padded straight stitch
Straight stitch
Spider web rose

SUPPLIES

Project
Purchased white Dupionni silk moneypurse
OR
One 24-inch square of white Dupionni silk
1 yard of ¼-inch double-sided white satin ribbon
20 inches of 2-inch gathered lace
White thread

Stitch Pattern
Page 140

Silk Ribbon
3 yards 4mm blue
1½ yards 4mm pink
1 yard 4mm bright green

Thread and Floss
1 skein blue embroidery floss (worked with three strands)
1 spool variegated green rayon thread *OR*
1 skein variegated green embroidery floss (worked with two strands)

Miscellaneous
Tracing paper
Permanent black fineline marker
Tulle netting
Water-soluble marking pen

This moneypurse, which can be used after the wedding as a lingerie bag, is adorned with a graceful bow that is stitched in an unusual way. Instead of filling the outline of the bow with satin stitches—a typical strategy for stitching large shapes—I echoed its curves with a series of spider web roses and padded straight stitch buds. The bow is used to secure a delicate bouquet of pink rosebuds, whose stems are stitched with variegated green thread or floss.

TRANSFER METHOD
Using the tulle netting transfer method (see page 24), lightly trace the design on the front of the moneypurse with the water-soluble marking pen. (If you're making your own purse, fold the silk in half wrong sides together, then trace the design on one side of the fabric.) After the stitching is complete, remove any visible marks with a damp cotton swab.

STITCHING INSTRUCTIONS
1. Stitch the stem stitch outline of the bow with blue embroidery floss.
2. Stitch the stem stitch stems with variegated green thread or floss.
3. Stitch the padded straight stitch rosebuds in the bouquet with pink silk ribbon.
4. Stitch the straight stitch leaves with green silk ribbon.
5. Stitch the spider web roses with blue silk ribbon, using the blue embroidery floss to make the foundation spokes.
6. Stitch the padded straight stitch rosebuds within the outline of the ribbon with blue silk ribbon.
7. Stitch the stem stitch and straight stitch stems and the straight stitch calyxes and stamens with variegated green thread or floss.

ASSEMBLING THE PURSE
If you're sewing your purse from a pattern, follow the instructions below.
1. Stitch a ⅜-inch fold at each end of the fabric to create a cinch pocket for the ribbon. Thread the satin ribbon through the pocket.
2. Lay the fabric wrong side down on your worktable. Pin the lace to the edge of the side seams. Fold the fabric right sides together, then stitch the side seams to the ribbon pocket.
3. Tie the ends of the ribbon together with a soft knot. Pull the ribbon to cinch the purse closed.

(Above) The completed moneypurse, with a detail of the padded ribbon stitch rosebuds and the spider web roses (right).

Christening Ensemble

SKILL LEVEL
Bib and bonnet: Beginner
Gown and shoes:
Intermediate

TIME TO COMPLETE
Gown: 60 hours
Bib: 1 to 2 hours
Bonnet: 2 hours
Shoes: 4 hours

STITCH PATTERNS
Page 141

STITCHES USED
Bradford rose
French knot
Padded straight stitch
Lazy daisy
Stem stitch
Straight stitch
Japanese ribbon stitch
(shoes only)

TRANSFER TOOLS
Tracing paper
Permanent black fineline
marker
Tulle netting
Water-soluble marking pen

CHRISTENING
GOWN SUPPLIES
Project
Purchased christening
gown (with matching slip)
Silk Ribbon
10 1/2 yards 4mm ivory
10 yards 4mm pink
5 yards 4mm banana
4 1/2 yards 4mm blue
3 yards 4mm green
2 yards 4mm rose red
1 1/2 yards 4mm lemon
yellow
Embroidery Floss
1 skein green floss
(worked with two strands)
Miscellaneous
4-inch hoop

*(See page 116 for bib,
bonnet, and shoes
supplies)*

Although this project requires a significant investment of time, most christening ceremonies are held when a baby is 3 to 12 months old, providing ample opportunity to complete the stitching over an extended period.

The long chain of stitches that I created for the gown I used for the demonstration actually consists of a series of four distinct designs that is repeated down the front of the garment. This arrangement allows you to work with any number or combination of the four designs, depending on the design of your gown.

Purchase the most expensive, well-constructed gown that you can afford in a natural-fiber fabric. The gown shown opposite is made of Swiss cotton batiste—a fine, sheer, plain-weave fabric—and has two vertical lace panels and a matching slip. I adapted the stitch motifs for a trio of satin accesories—bib, bonnet, and shoes—but the gown's designs can also be worked as a border on a baby blanket or christening pillow.

If properly stored, this gown and its accessories can become family heirlooms, to be worn by baby girls for many years to come. (For more information, see "Storing Your Projects," page 28.) The shoes can be framed in a shadowbox, along with the baby's silver rattle, a lock of her hair, and photographs of her special day.

TRANSFER METHODS
- *For the gown, bib, and shoes.* Use the water-soluble marking pen to mark the centers of the Bradford roses, the lazy daisy and French knot flowers, and the paths of the stems.
- *For the bonnet.* Using the tulle netting transfer method (see page 24), lightly trace the design on the fabric with the water-soluble marking pen. To reverse the design to stitch the other side of the bonnet, trace the design on tracing paper with a black fineline marker. Turn the traced design face down, then trace it on tulle netting with the black marker. Pin the netting to the bonnet and trace the design on the fabric with a water-soluble pen.

After the stitching is complete, remove any visible marks with a damp cotton swab.

STITCHING INSTRUCTIONS

GOWN
The following step-by-step progression of stitches applies to all four stitch designs. Begin at the top of the lace panel and work the designs sequentially to the bottom of the skirt. To prevent excessive creasing, remove the hoop when you're done stitching for the day.

1. Using rose red silk ribbon for the French knot centers and pink silk ribbon for the surrounding whip stitches, stitch the Bradford roses.
2. Stitch the padded straight stitch buds with pink silk ribbon.
3. Stitch the lazy daisy leaves with green silk ribbon.
4. Stitch the stem stitches and the straight stitch calyxes and stamens that accent the buds with green embroidery floss.
5. Stitch the French knot forget-me-nots with blue (for the petals) and lemon yellow (for the centers) silk ribbons.
6. Stitch the lazy daisy flowers with banana silk ribbon. Add a French knot center to each with pink silk ribbon.
7. Stitch the scattered French knots with a single wrap of ivory silk ribbon.

The complete christening ensemble: gown, bonnet, shoes, and bib.

BIB SUPPLIES

Project

Purchased lace bib

Silk Ribbon

1½ yards 4mm ivory

16 inches 4mm pink

16 inches 4mm green

16 inches 4mm blue

16 inches 4mm banana

8 inches 4mm rose red

8 inches 4mm lemon yellow

Embroidery Floss

1 skein green (worked with two strands)

BONNET SUPPLIES

Project

Purchased christening bonnet with lace trim

Silk Ribbon

2 yards 4mm ivory

1 yard 4mm pink

1 yard 4mm green

1 yard 4mm blue

1 yard 4mm banana

8 inches 4mm rose red

8 inches 4mm lemon yellow

Embroidery Floss

1 skein green (worked with two strands)

SHOES SUPPLIES

Project

Purchased satin christening shoes

Silk Ribbon

1 yard 4mm pink

1 yard 4mm ivory

24 inches 4mm rose red

24 inches 4mm green

24 inches 4mm blue

24 inches 4mm banana

10 inches 4mm lemon yellow

Satin Ribbon

16 inches 1-inch double-sided pink

Thread and Floss

1 skein green (worked with two strands)

1 spool white thread

Miscellaneous

Fray Check

BIB AND BONNET

To stitch either the bib or the bonnet, repeat steps 1 through 7 on page 114. (Note that the bonnet design should be stitched on both sides of the bonnet.)

SHOES

1. Using rose red silk ribbon for the French knot centers and pink silk ribbon for the surrounding whip stitches, stitch the Bradford rose on the top of each shoe.
2. On the sides and soles of the shoes, stitch the lazy daisy flowers with rose red, banana, and blue silk ribbons. Add a contrasting French knot center to each flower with lemon yellow, blue, or rose red silk ribbon.
3. Stitch the Japanese ribbon stitch and lazy daisy leaves with green silk ribbon.
4. Stitch the stem stitches with green embroidery floss.
5. Stitch the French knot forget-me-nots with blue (for the petals) and lemon yellow (for the centers) silk ribbons.
6. Stitch the scattered French knots with a single wrap of ivory silk ribbon.
7. Cut the pink satin ribbon into two 8-inch lengths, then tie each into a bow. Use the white thread and tiny stitches to tack one bow to the strap of each shoe. Cut the ribbon ends to sharply angled points, then coat the ends with Fray Check.

The bib (opposite), the bonnet (right), and the shoes (below), with a detail of the sole (below right).

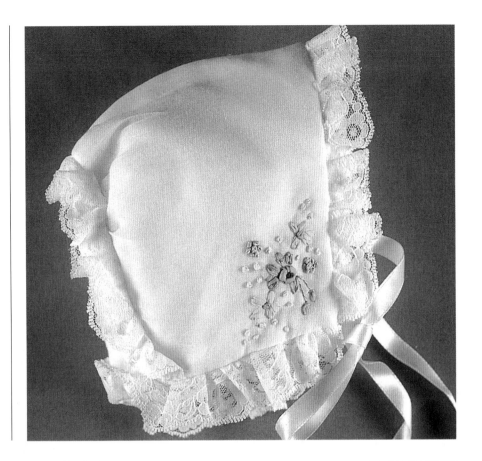

Stitch Patterns

On pages 119–141 are the stitch patterns for the 35 projects in this book. The stitch key below indicates the symbols that are used to represent each of the 22 stitches as well as two types of embellishments. For your convenience, all of the patterns are reproduced at actual size. Trace each of the patterns as you need them onto a piece of tracing paper with a pencil or a black fineline marker, then refer to the project instructions for the recommended transfer method. For a discussion of various transfer techniques, see "Pattern Transfer Tools," page 24.

STITCH KEY

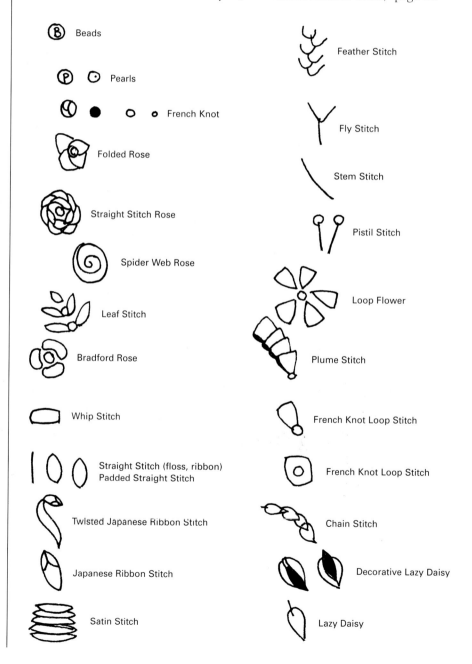

Beads

Pearls

French Knot

Folded Rose

Straight Stitch Rose

Spider Web Rose

Leaf Stitch

Bradford Rose

Whip Stitch

Straight Stitch (floss, ribbon)
Padded Straight Stitch

Twisted Japanese Ribbon Stitch

Japanese Ribbon Stitch

Satin Stitch

Feather Stitch

Fly Stitch

Stem Stitch

Pistil Stitch

Loop Flower

Plume Stitch

French Knot Loop Stitch

French Knot Loop Stitch

Chain Stitch

Decorative Lazy Daisy

Lazy Daisy

LINEN HANDKERCHIEF
See pages 54–55 for project instructions.

BATTENBERG LACE EYEGLASS CASE
See pages 56–57 for project instructions.

FRINGED SILK PURSE
See pages 58–59 for project instructions.

SILK EVENING BAG
See pages 62–63 for project instructions.

INFANT CUFF CAP AND MITTENS
See pages 66–67 for project instructions.

Mittens

Cuff cap

TODDLER "BUBBLE" ENSEMBLE

See pages 68–69 for project instructions.

Right

Right collar (reverse pattern for left collar)

Slippers (front of shoe)

Pockets

Left

Bonnet

LINEN BLOUSE
See pages 70–71 for project instructions.

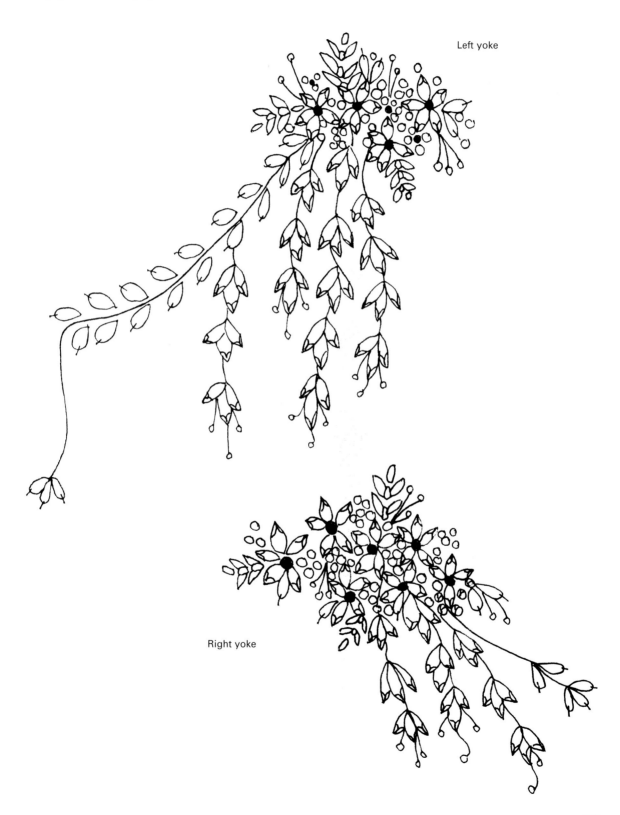

Left yoke

Right yoke

SILKEN CAMISOLE AND TAP PANT

See pages 72–73 for project instructions.

COTTON CHAMBRAY JUMPER

(below and opposite)
See pages 74–75 for
project instructions.

Tap pant

Design 2: Left shoulder

Right side of camisole
(reverse pattern for left side)

DAMASK WAISTCOAT

(below, opposite, and on page 128)
See pages 76–77 for project instructions.

Vest point, right

Vest point, left

Top

Back neckline

Right side, from back
to top buttonhole

Buttonhole

Waistcoat closure
between buttons

DAMASK WAISTCOAT
(below and on pages 126–127)
See pages 76–77 for project instructions.

Left side, from back
to top button

BROCADE VEST

(below and on page 130)
See pages 78–81 for project instructions.

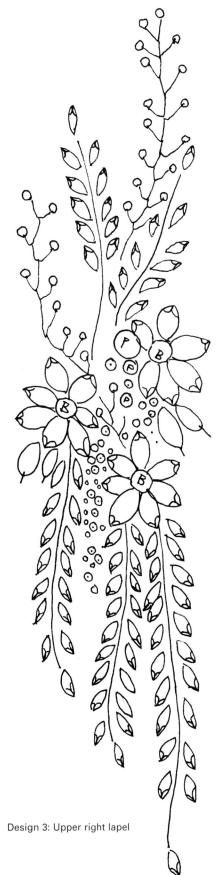

Design 1: Upper left lapel

Design 3: Upper right lapel

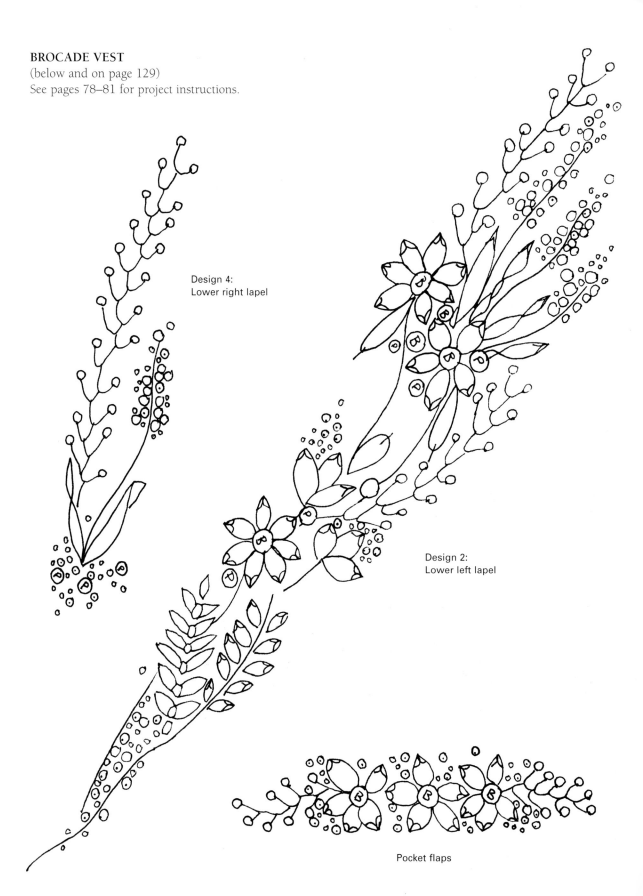

BROCADE VEST
(below and on page 129)
See pages 78–81 for project instructions.

Design 4:
Lower right lapel

Design 2:
Lower left lapel

Pocket flaps

BROCADE SACHET
See pages 84–85 for project instructions.

PORCELAIN JAR WITH MOIRÉ COVER
See pages 86–87 for project instructions.

EYELET LAMPSHADE
See pages 88–89 for project instructions.

TASSELED MOIRÉ AND LACE PILLOW
(below and opposite)
See pages 90–91 for project instructions.

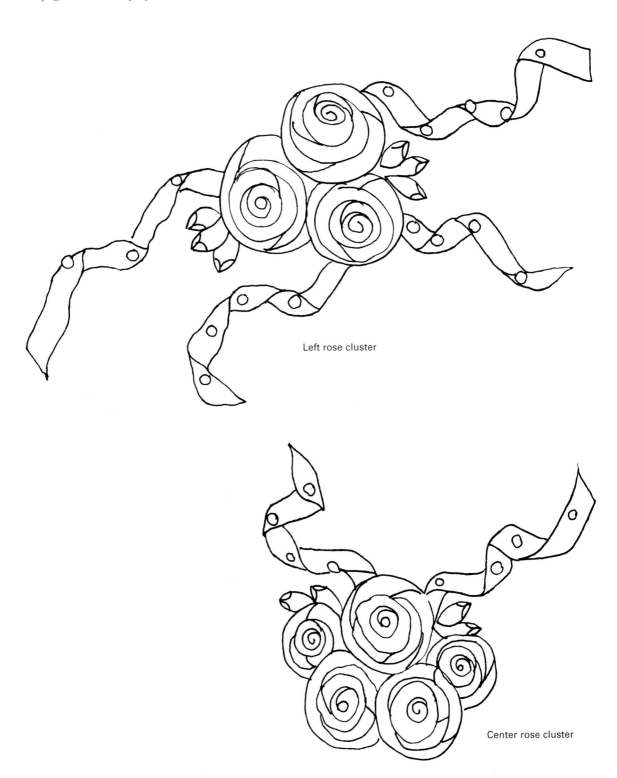

Left rose cluster

Center rose cluster

Right rose cluster

DAMASK HAND MIRROR

See pages 94–95 for project instructions.

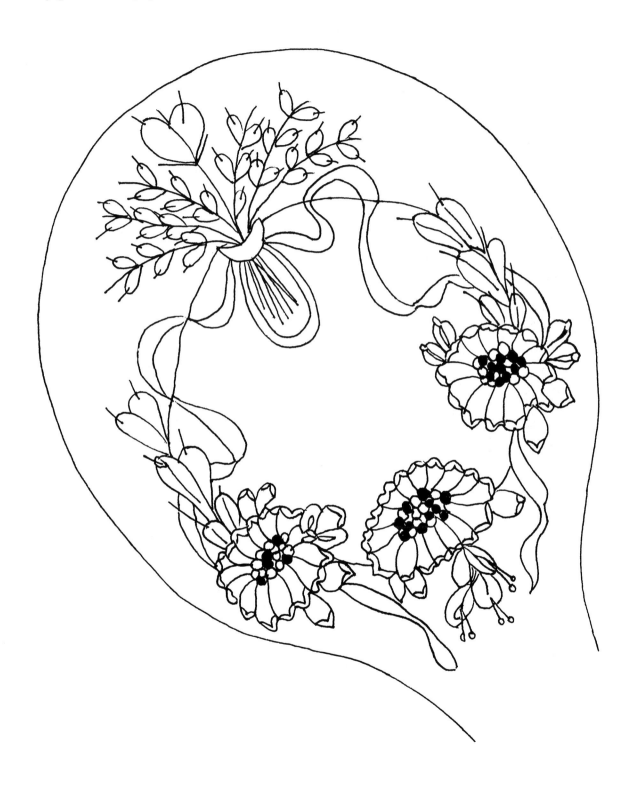

● = French knots stitched with ecru floss

FRAMED DRESDEN VASE

See pages 98–101 for project instructions.

R = Folded rose

L = French knot loop stitch

CHRISTMAS ORNAMENTS
See pages 104–107 for project instructions.

Heart

Bell

Boot

BRIDAL SACHET
See pages 108–109 for project instructions.

RINGBEARER'S PILLOW
See pages 110–111 for project instructions.

CHRISTENING ENSEMBLE

See pages 114–117 for project instructions.

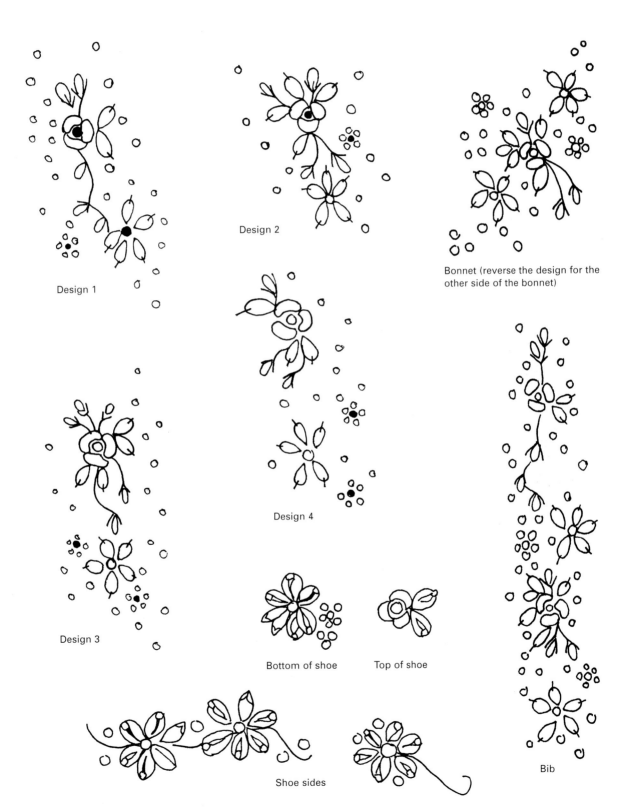

Design 1

Design 2

Bonnet (reverse the design for the other side of the bonnet)

Design 3

Design 4

Bottom of shoe

Top of shoe

Shoe sides

Bib

Source Directory

Listed at right are the manufacturers and wholesale suppliers for many of the materials used in this book. These companies sell their products exclusively to sewing and notions, fabric, needlearts, craft, and hobby retailers, which are a consumer's most dependable sources for silk ribbon embroidery supplies. Your local retailer's knowledgeable personnel can advise you on your purchases, and if you need something they don't have in stock they will usually order it for you. If you can't find a store in your area that carries a particular item or will accept a request for an order, or if you need special assistance, a manufacturer will gladly direct you to the retailer nearest you that carries their products and will try to answer any other questions you might have. If you've exhausted all these avenues and still can't find what you're looking for, contact some of the mail-order sources at the end of the list.

MANUFACTURERS AND WHOLESALE DISTRIBUTORS

SILK AND SYNTHETIC RIBBON

Ribbon Connection
969 Industrial Road – Suite E
San Carlos, California 94707
(415) 593-5221/FAX (415) 593-6785

WFR Ribbon, Inc.
259 Center Street
Phillipsburg, New Jersey 08865-3397
(908) 454-7700/FAX (908) 454-0657
Exclusive U.S. distributor of Mokuba synthetic ribbons

YLI Corporation
P.O. Box 109
Provo, Utah 84603-0109
(801) 377-3900/FAX (801) 375-2879

VARIEGATED SILK RIBBON

Yarn Barn of San Antonio
4300 McCullough
San Antonio, Texas 78212
(210) 826-3679/FAX (210) 826-6722

THREAD AND FLOSS

Coats & Clark
Department CO1
P.O. Box 27067
Greenville, South Carolina 29616
(803) 234-0331

The DMC Corporation
10 Port Kearny
South Kearny, New Jersey 07032-4688

Kreinik Manufacturing Company, Inc.
3106 Timanus Lane – Suite 101
Baltimore, Maryland 21244
(410) 581-5088/FAX (410) 581-5092

EMBELLISHMENTS

Creative Beginnings
475 Morro Bay Boulevard
Morro Bay, California 93442
(805) 772-6315

Gay Bowles Sales, Inc.
P.O. Box 1060
Janesville, Wisconsin 53547
(608) 754-9212/FAX (608) 754-0665

PROJECT SUPPLIES

Folkwear Patterns
Taunton Press
63 South Main Street
P.O. Box 5506
Newtown, Connecticut 06470-5506
Pattern for Broadcloth Tea Cozy, pages 92–93

Home Arts
2101 Fifth Avenue
Atwater, California 95301
(800) 484-9923; PIN #2787
Kit for Damask Hand Mirror, pages 94–95

JanLynn Corporation
34 Front Street
Indian Orchard, Massachusetts 51848
(413) 543-7500/FAX (413) 543-7505
Cotton Chambray Jumper, pages 74–75

Novtex/Land O'Lace
510 State Road
North Adams, Massachusetts 01247
(413) 664-4509/FAX (413) 663-5780
Lace for Eyelet Lampshade, pages 88–89

Pres-On Merchandising Corp.
1020 South Westgate Drive
Addison, Illinois 60101
(708) 543-9370/FAX (708) 543-9406
Shapes for Christmas Ornaments, pages 104–107

Sara's Bloom
36 Rainbow Lake
Irvine, California 92714
(714) 651-8484/FAX (714) 651-8435
Fringed Silk Purse, pages 58–59
Silk Evening Bag, pages 62–63

Wimpole Street, Inc.
P.O. Box 395
West Bountiful, Utah 84087
(801) 298-0504/FAX (801) 298-1333
Lace for Battenberg Lace Eyeglass Case, pages 56–57

Zweigart Fabrics and Canvas
Weston Canal Plaza
2 Riverview Drive
Somerset, New Jersey 08873-1139
(908) 271-1948/FAX (908) 271-0758
Fabrics for Damask Waistcoat, pages 76–77 and Damask Hand Mirror, pages 94–95

MISCELLANEOUS SUPPLIES

Adhesive Technologies, Inc.
3 Merrill Industrial Drive
Hampton, New Hampshire 03842-1995
(603) 926-1616/FAX (603) 926-1780
Glue guns and glue sticks

Berroco, Inc.
14 Elmdale Road
Uxbridge, Massachusetts 01569-0367
(508) 278-2527/FAX (508) 278-2461
Distributor of Handeze Craft Gloves

June Tailor, Inc.
P.O. Box 208
Richfield, Wisconsin 53076-0208
(800) 844-5400/FAX (800) 246-1573
Manufacturer of Velvaboard

Mini Magic
3910 Patricia Drive
Columbus, Ohio 43220
(614) 457-3805/FAX (614) 459-2306
Acid-free boxes and tissues; doll-size ironing boards

Quilter's Resource
P.O. Box 148850
Chicago, Illinois 60614
(312) 278-5695/FAX (312) 278-1348
General sewing supplies, trims, and kits

MAIL ORDER SOURCES

SILK RIBBON

Angelsea
P.O. Box 4586
Stockton, California 95204
(209) 948-8428

Elf Design Studio
5013 50th Street
P.O. Box 3883
Olds, Alberta, Canada T4H1P6
(403) 556-3999/FAX (403) 556-1686

Evening Star Designs
69 Coolidge Avenue
Haverhill, Massachusetts 01832
(508) 372-3473

Lacis
2982 Adeline Street
Berkeley, California 94703
(510) 843-7178/FAX (510) 843-5018

Sandy's Ribbons and Laces
7417 North Knoxville
Peoria, Illinois 61614
(309) 689-1943 (phone and FAX)

Sherry's Shallie
8732 Haskell Street
Riverside, California 92503
(909) 688-5471

Textile Reproductions
P.O. Box 48
West Chesterfield, Massachusetts 01084
(413) 296-4437

Things Japanese
9805 N.E. 116th Street – Suite 7160
Kirkland, Washington 98034
(206) 821-2287 (phone and FAX)

GENERAL SEWING SUPPLIES

Clotilde, Inc.
2 Sew Smart Way B8031
Stevens Point, Wisconsin 54481-8031
(800) 772-2891/FAX (715) 341-3082

Dawn's Discount Lace II
8655 Sepulveda Boulevard
Los Angeles, California 90045
(310) 641-3466/FAX (310) 641-1211

Elsie's Exquisiques
208 State Street
St. Joseph, Michigan 49085
(616) 982-0449/FAX (616) 982-0963

Nancy's Notions
333 Beichl Avenue
P.O. Box 683
Beaver Dam, Wisconsin 53916-0683
(800) 833-0690/FAX (800) 255-8119

VINTAGE AND HISTORICAL KITS AND PATTERNS

RibbonSmyth
P.O. Box 416
Fountainville, Pennsylvania 18923
(215) 249-1258/FAX (215) 249-3628

Index